UNACCOUNTED

MICHAEL MCDONALD-LOW

The true story

of an American infantryman

MIA in one of Vietnam's deadliest locations

and the mission to find him forty-four years later

First Edition Design Publishing

Unaccounted

Copyright ©2015 Michael McDonald -Low

ISBN 978-1506-900-89-6 PRINT
ISBN 978-1506-900-90-2 EBOOK

LCCN 2015958996

December 2015

Published and Distributed by
First Edition Design Publishing, Inc.
P.O. Box 20217, Sarasota, FL 34276-3217
www.firsteditiondesignpublishing.com

www.unaccounted.net

DELTA SIX PRODUCTIONS, LLC
Cover Design: Sheridan K. Low

Warning: This book contains explicit language.

DEDICATION

Unaccounted is dedicated to
Clifford D. Van Artsdalen – MIA 1165,
to the many other soldiers who remain MIA,
and to my infantry veteran brothers
in arms who lived and died
for their country and fellow soldiers.

No higher commitment.
No greater loyalty.

Table of Contents

PROLOGUE

Over 83,000 American military personnel are still missing in action (MIA); officially listed as killed in action - body not recovered. They rest in unmarked graves in foreign countries or in watery tombs out at sea. 73,515 are from World War II, 7,852 are from the Korean War and over 1,600 remain unaccounted for in Vietnam. Their families, brothers-in-arms, and Americans everywhere yearn for their discovery and return to United States soil.

The search for American MIAs began at the conclusion of the Vietnam War when the parents of those veterans reported missing in action demanded an accounting for their sons. Today, bringing closure to all families of lost soldiers from all conflicts has become one of America's most important and compassionate missions.

The Joint POW/MIA Accounting Command and the Defense Prisoner of War/Missing Personnel Office (DPMO) are joint task forces within the United States Department of Defense whose mission is to account for Americans who are listed as Prisoners Of War or Missing in Action. Since the writing of this book, JPAC and DPMO have been combined into a new, more streamlined and integrated agency; the

Defense POW/MIA Accounting Agency – DPAA. All e-mails between me, JPAC and DPMO are representative of actual unclassified communications. The names of all JPAC and DPMO personnel have been changed to protect their identities.

All views expressed in this book are my own and are not those of the Department of Defense or any of its agencies.

All excerpts from historical After-Action Reports are presented as written by the reporting units.

The men portrayed herein as members of Delta Company, 1st Battalion, 20th Infantry, 11th Light Infantry Brigade and other infantry units are representative of the men of those units as a whole. I have no desire to expose any man who may suffer from Post-Traumatic Stress Disorder or any family that has lost a loved one, so I have changed the names and identifying characteristics of the soldiers portrayed in this book. In certain instances, I have altered the job duties some soldiers might have originally fulfilled in Vietnam, specifically because it did not contribute to or alter the overall accuracy of the story, and in the end we all ended up as infantry grunts. It was also impossible to mention every member of the units listed.

I have taken the liberty of writing for Clifford Van Artsdalen (officially designated by the Defense Department as MIA 1165) in the first person, because I deeply believe this is his story as much as it is mine. I also wanted to bring him to life so readers would better understand his perspective, duties and combat experiences as that of an enlisted infantry soldier who always tried to do his best. His narrative and portrayal are from my recollections and he is representative of the men serving at that time.

There are no "John Wayne" heroes portrayed in this story; the everyday acts by the infantrymen of Delta Company reflected the day-to-day sacrifice, heroic service, and battlefield mentality by that group of men during that period of United States military history.

The events described in this book are true, but are not intended to be a word-for-word, day-by-day, bullet-by-bullet documentation; rather, they are intended to capture the essence of the moment and the experience. The actions and incidents I have described are from my memories supported by After-Action Reports, research and data gleaned from other books, internet resources, and interviews with other soldiers, including some former North Vietnamese Army officers. The dialogue presented herein reflects that era of time, (i.e. most of the nation including the Armed Services had not yet been conditioned to use the terms Black or Afro-American). Any errors made in this story are unintentional and likely can be attributed to the passage of time and the nature of infantry combat in Vietnam.

Please refer to the Glossary of Vietnam Terminology to better understand some commonly used abbreviations, terms, and expressions.

INTRODUCTION

In the northern provinces of South Vietnam, the Que Son Valley AO (Area of Operations) included the Hiep Duc Valley and the adjoining Que Son Valley to its west. These two valleys were one of the first natural passageways to South Vietnam for North Vietnamese Army (NVA) soldiers coming down the Ho Chi Minh Trail from North Vietnam and Laos. Surrounding the valleys was a morass of hills and 9,850-foot tall mountains covered with dense jungle growth reaching double and triple canopy height. It was in these concealed mountainous areas that the 2nd NVA Division established their regimental strongholds and from where they staged and launched their attacks on American and South Vietnamese forces.

The 300 square miles of the Que Son Valley AO was a very bad place with a very bad reputation. More U.S. Army infantrymen and Marines died there than at any other location in Vietnam. More Medals of Honor were awarded in this region than in any other single combat location. The U.S. Marines, 1st Air Cavalry Division, and 101st Airborne Division had all fought there since 1965.

From 12 February 1968 to 17 April 1968, U.S. Army infantry units under the operational control of the Americal Division's 196th Light Infantry Brigade, inflicted grave punishment upon regiments of the 2nd NVA Division in the Que Son Valley AO, but at a great cost with more than 900 U.S. casualties reported. On 19 April 1968, the 198th Light Infantry Brigade assumed operational control from the 196th in the AO. The infantry units under their command included the 1st Battalion, 20th Infantry of the 11th Brigade, and their own 1st Battalion, 6th Infantry and 1st Battalion, 52nd Infantry.

On 5 May 1968, the downing of two helicopters in the Que Son Valley, near the 198th's firebase at LZ Center, marked the beginning of the North Vietnamese Army's second Tet offensive and their goal of destroying all U.S. forces. At 1728 hours, Delta Company, 1st Battalion, 20th Infantry conducted a combat air assault to join Bravo Company, 1st Battalion, 6th Infantry at the helicopters' fatally downed location. Their experiences during the next six days set the stage for a three-month long battle that lasted only hours for some. In the end, there would be more than 2,300 dead and wounded, and one American Soldier missing in action. It will take over 44 years to find his location; UNACCOUNTED is his story.

PART ONE

CROSSBOW DELTA

The tragedy of war is that it uses man's best to do man's worst.

Harry Emerson Fosdick

Chapter 1

JUST LAST NIGHT

Narrative: *M. McDonald-Low*

June 2009

Heavy rain beat against my bedroom window and it startled me awake, momentarily pausing my dream. My heart was pounding. I was in a cold sweat. I rolled over and looked at the shadows of the trees as they danced and swayed against the rain swept window. The sound reminded me of another time in the rain. I calmed my thoughts, closed my eyes, and listened to the rain and my breathing. My mind slowed and I drifted back to a place I had been many times before, to see whether there was a change I could have made, a circumstance I missed, or a fault I didn't recognize making. I relaxed and slowly fell back to sleep, returning to that day in 1968.

I had to duck to get through the small opening to the trail that was partially concealed by large banana leafed plants and palms of bamboo. The trail was barely three feet wide with thick brush, scrub trees, bamboo, giant ferns, elephant ear plants, and vine entanglements on either side. On the east side of the trail, a narrow rock embankment about eighteen inches high marked the edge of a dry streambed that was about ten feet wide.

Given the dangers of the location and terrain, we moved slow and deliberate in single file, spread-out every ten to fifteen feet. The North Vietnamese Army had made no secret of their strength here. This was their home turf and base camp, and they were willing to stand and fight to keep it. More than that, they were committed to inflicting as much carnage and death on those American infantry units who dared oppose them here in their mountain fortresses in the Que Son Valley.

My dream jerked and stuttered forward like an old silent movie.

After a while, it seemed we were always trudging and plowing our way out of the rice paddies heading uphill; we were following the rain fed streams that ran down from the mountains. When I looked at our topography maps, it was easy to pinpoint trouble and potential hotspots in our area of operations. We all knew the NVA were coming down from their strongholds in the mountains towards us, or lying in wait near streams that ran down from the many ridges and hilltops that stretched to the populous valleys and flatlands of the coast.

Water also meant leeches.

The brown leeches were everywhere and as if by magic, they clung to our boots, gear, clothing, and skin. Dirty little bastards, they methodically looked for openings in our clothing and boots gravitating to the warmth of our body. Inching forward, leeches were as relentless as they were stealthy. You rarely recognized them until you had ten attached to you, or you discovered a bloodstain beginning to bloom on your uniform.

I remembered using my cigarette to burn a big, fat, brownish-red, blood-engorged leech off my arm as I watched my radioman Macintyre squirt mosquito repellant on several leeches that had attached to his boots. He then passed me the repellant and I doused my boots. I watched the leeches fall off, writhing from the liquid.

"Your head is bleeding again, LT."

I hadn't noticed, but when I reached up to my forehead, I could feel that the wound pad covering the gash was wet. When I pulled my hand back, my fingers were smeared with blood.

I looked at Mac, "Are the stitches coming loose?"

Macintyre looked at my forehead carefully and turned my head to the right and left as he peaked under the gauze pad. "No, I don't think so, but your forehead is definitely swollen and bleeding. It looks like shit, LT. There's a small flap of

5

skin that has opened near one of the pieces of tape and that's where the blood is coming from, but it hasn't torn all the way open."

"Okay, okay, I'm good," I said, patting my forehead with the back of my sleeve. I really didn't have the luxury of time to stop and do anything about the oozing blood.

Ahead of me, Van Artsdalen and Zapata were on point with five others behind them. They had led the platoon and company up the trail. It had been raining on and off all morning. We were soaked. Macintyre had come up from behind me and tapped me on the elbow to let me know I had a call on the radio. That's when we had both noticed the leeches.

When Mac passed me the telephone handset that ran from a coiled, black cord to the top of the radio strapped to his back, it was automatic for the movement of the platoon to stop; hand signals and whispers would go up and down trail. The whole company would gradually lurch to a stop behind us. Spread out like we were, it took a while for the entire column to come to a complete stop.

Passing the repellant back to Macintyre, I put the handset to my ear and spoke into the receiver, "One Six, go."

"What's the hold up, One Six?" It was Sonata, my company commander.

"Six, there is no hold up. We're just taking our time up here. It's slow, wet, and I really don't want to hurry on this trail, over."

"One Six, we have our asses hanging out all over these village hooches and open areas. We need to get moving. Do you roger?"

"One Six, I roger. We'll step it up, out."

I passed the handset back to Macintyre. I looked ahead to Lockhart, and in a low whisper said, "Pass it up and tell Van Artsdalen everything is good. Let's keep it rolling. Everyone is cluster fucked behind us in the village."

Lockhart, who was calmly smoking, his M16 held in the crook of his arm, nodded at me and gave me the thumbs up. All good.

Thirty seconds later we started our climb again in that herky-jerky, stop and go infantry style we all loved.

I wasn't real happy. I had been ordered to break the rules and follow the trail leading up the hill towards LZ Center. I wasn't comfortable with the order, because I knew the NVA would be hanging close to us, trying to slow us down and stop us from reaching the safe confines of the fire support base. I also knew that Sonata was in a hurry and he had been told to make haste in that particular direction, "Quickest possible route," is what he said to me. I still felt that he was pressing me to hurry too quickly on a trail I knew could be trouble. I didn't like it, but I quickly dumped the thought. It was my job to get us there. Enough said.

The numerous casualties from our six days of combat on Hill 352 hung on the men, their expressions a mix of anguish and dread. It wasn't so much fear as it was the speculation that something terrible was about to happen. The unexpected had occurred so frequently here that each soldier hoped it didn't happen to him. I watched as their backs bent and their shoulders sloped forward under the enormous weight of the water, ammo, gear and weapons. The 100% humidity and cloying heat of the jungle had each of us in a dead sweat and it was just 0800 hours. The standing joke among us was that the insidious heat was a constant reminder that we were all in hell.

We moved without talking, one well-placed step at a time, focused on the trail as it continued its serpentine climb heading for Hill 348 and LZ Center, 1,142 feet from the rice paddied floor of the valley below.

The images of my dream fast-forwarded, stopped, and then continued.

I remembered Mac and me pushing Sonata and his RTO, Jenkins, over the small rocks at the edge of the streambed when we heard the big NVA machine gun go off, rounds ripping the ground around us. When we landed, I was practically on top of Sonata face to face. His helmet had been knocked off. We both looked at each other and I said, "That was close."

Sonata nodded at me and in a calm voice said, "Mike, get'em up and moving or we are dead meat."

I rolled away from Sonata, crawled back and peaked above the rock wall. Macintyre had also regrouped and was beside me. I couldn't see a damn thing, but the machine gun had momentarily stopped firing. Taking advantage of the pause, we stood up, jumped over the wall and with our M16's in hand started running down trail passing some soldiers who were just starting to raise their heads. I yelled at them to return fire as we ran past. I had one thing on my mind and that was to get back to the rest of my platoon and get them moving. Moments later the chaos of the ambush erupted again behind us. Mac and I grabbed some dirt and flattened out.

Time slowed.

Men littered the trail. Doc Nelson had fallen and was just sitting there with an eighteen-inch long spring of an M16 magazine protruding out of either side of his chest bobbing up and down. I said something when I ran up to him, but I didn't know what. Across from Nelson, Cerutti had a big bloodstain on his pant leg, but he was up and blasting away with his M60. The spent shell casings from his machine gun spewed out in a golden arc, landing on his two ammo bearers who were lying wounded or dead at his feet. Down trail from Cerutti, two other men were spread eagle and face down on either side of the trail. Their steel pots were lying next to them and their M16's were held in lifeless hands. Both had bloody, gaping holes that had burst from the backs of their jungle shirts. I saw others down trail from them hunkering down behind rocks and brush, dazed and in shock from the heavy machine gun, AK47 fire, and grenades that were exploding from the "Y."

The screams for "Medic!" had begun.

I jumped involuntarily. Beads of sweat covered my forehead. My heart was pounding. It startled and surprised me every single time, the nightmare of 11 May 1968.

I paused and let out my breath. I looked carefully, my head motionless on the pillow. I was searching the shadows on the window for any aberrant movement or shift in their shape. "It was the subtleties that killed you," I thought.

My hyper-vigilance was on overdrive. I had the big ears on, too. That just came with the whole PTSD package.

I listened, quietly. I attempted to subdue my breathing so I could hear the smallest of creaks. New houses were the worst. The home I lived in now was like an arthritic old crone, though it was only ten years old. It groaned. It popped. It would snap like a bare foot with a broken toe on a hardwood floor. On windy, rainy nights like tonight, it was always worse. It took me much longer to decipher the added thumps and scrapes of the trees against the side of the house. It was always on a west wind off the coast.

"Nothing. Nothing to worry about," I thought as I laughed under my breath.

It was an old joke. I had heard it before. The psychiatrist turned to the veteran and said, "Tell me son, when was the last time you were in Vietnam?"

The man paused and looked at the doctor, "Just last night."

The memories of war can haunt you for a lifetime and I had been there again tonight for the 14,965th time in a row. I poured over the details and I checked and rechecked my memories of that day.

I was pretty damn sure someone had made a big mistake.

Chapter 2

FIRST REAL CONTACT

M. McDonald-Low

2010

EMAIL

Michael McDonald-Low to Defense Prisoner of War/Missing Personnel Office (DPMO)

13 June 2010

Dear Sir,

I am a former platoon leader and company commander of Delta Company, 1st Battalion, 20th Infantry, 11th Light Infantry Brigade. I served in Vietnam in 1967 and 1968. In 2009, I noticed an error on the 1/20 Infantry website. The information listed Specialist 4 Clifford Van Artsdalen as an MIA/KHA on May 9, 1968, at Nui Hoac Ridge, vicinity Hill 352. Both the date and location are incorrect. I reported this to the Joint POW/MIA Accounting Agency (JPAC) previously in 2009.

UNACCOUNTED

I would like to provide new coordinates and info on Van Artsdalen. He was a member of my platoon. My memories are particularly clear because I was there on the day he died and I was also wounded that day, May 11th.

I have seen the JPAC photos from their 2007 search and I know they do not have the right location. Van Artsdalen fought on Hill 352, but he wasn't killed there. We were en route to LZ Center when the incident occurred. I have been with many guys back in country who were "close" on maps, but you wouldn't want to use their coordinates to shoot artillery there.

If I can help, contact me.

Michael McDonald-Low

———

EMAIL

Holmes, Catherine, Capt. USAF, DPMO to Michael McDonald-Low

14 June 2010

Mr. McDonald-Low,

Thank you so very much for your information, and most importantly, thank you for your service and sacrifice.

I would like to take a day or so to review all of the information you sent me, compare it with the documents I have here and gather my thoughts/questions. Then if you don't mind, I would like to talk it over with you to see if we can figure out where all of our wires got crossed.

I can give you one bit of insight as to where the date confusion is coming in. In the files we have here at DPMO, we have the statements from the 20 May 1968 board of inquiry from Cpt. Charles S. Sonata, Commanding Officer, Company D, 1-20th Infantry.

His statements place the date/time the loss at approximately 1300 hours, 9 May 1968, in the vicinity of grid coordinates 074227. By no means am I closed to the possibility that the information could be incorrect, but the boards of inquiry documents have served as primary sources determining the date and location of loss for Sp.4 Clifford Van Artsdalen – MIA 1165.

Again, I thank you very much. I welcome any information you can offer.

Catherine Holmes, Capt, USAF

———

EMAIL

Michael McDonald-Low to Catherine Holmes, Capt. USAF, DPMO

15 June 2010

Thanks for writing me back.

It is funny that Sonata could be so wrong, but he was and he admitted it to me when I visited with him last February. As Van Artsdalen's platoon leader I was the one who specifically sent him up that trail on May 11. The same day AND time I was wounded. That's why it is so ingrained in me. It is hard to forget things like that.

You may contact me at your leisure. I am retired and generally at home.

Michael McDonald-Low

―――――

EMAIL

Holmes, Catherine, Capt. USAF, DPMO to Michael McDonald-Low

18 June 2010

Mr. McDonald-Low,

I have contacted Mr. Ray Carne, an analyst from JPAC, (Joint Prisoners of War, Missing in Action Accounting Command). He will drop a hard copy map in the mail for you today. If you would, please mark the location the team should search and return the map to Ray at JPAC. If you could also include any additional descriptive details of the terrain and loss location to help the team narrow down the area. That would be most helpful.

Once again, thank you so very much for your service, and for taking the time to work with us to hopefully resolve SP4 Van Artsdalen's case. Please do not hesitate to contact Ray or me if you have any additional questions or information.

Catherine Holmes, Capt. USAF

————

EMAIL

Carne, Ray Civ JPAC J2 to Michael McDonald-Low

18 June 2010

Mr. McDonald-Low,

My name is Ray Carne and I'm with JPAC. I am sending a 1:50,000 map this afternoon (Hawaii time) for you to indicate on the map the location where we need to look.

Please call my office as soon as you have the grid coordinates.

From this point forward we will refer to Clifford Van Artsdalen as 1165.

I appreciate all that you are doing for us.

Ray Carne

————

EMAIL

Michael McDonald-Low to Carne, Ray Civ JPAC J2 and Holmes, Catherine, Capt DPMO

20 June 2010

Mr. Carne and Ms. Holmes,

Thanks for the map. I have indicated the locations of where our LZ was located and where the two choppers were shot down (C1 & C2). I have also circled the area where 1165 was lost. I can be more specific with better maps.

Best,

Michael

Chapter 3

RESURRECTION

Narrative: *Clifford Van Artsdalen – MIA 1165*

9 March 2012

It began very slowly for me: a small tic, a subtle breeze of awareness, a growing sensation of the here and now, as well as the past.

It had been a long time since I had experienced anything. My surroundings were more a blurred image of the past than they were of a physical presence, dark and green. The matte of vines, shrubs, banana plants, bamboo, ferns and the wild perverse growth of what was the jungle hung heavily on me; like the humidity, I wore it like a shroud. Only shadows and faint light penetrated the canopies, contributing to the oppression.

This morning I felt disconcerted. Cold. For the first time in a long time I felt something and I began to remember; a picture puzzle of a thousand disconnected, but related pieces. Waking. Thoughts of my boyhood in Kentucky were disjointed and vague: the smell of my parent's home, the laughter of my sister, my mother's smile, a golden trail that led up a green hillside. My attentions seemed fleeting, blurred in my consciousness and were as random as the mist on the mountainous hillsides of the Que Son Valley. Most mornings the mist was burned quickly away as the sun turned the lush green land hot and humid. On other days it would persist, prolonging the chill of another dank morning in the jungles of the high ridgelines and hills.

I wasn't quite aware of the why or the how, and my thoughts were still new and crowded, but I remembered going to high school and killing time waiting to get out, and not sure of anything but that, just getting out. I had no idea what or whom I was to become, but I knew it had a lot to do with leaving Plumsteadville, Pennsylvania. I couldn't seem to please anyone, not my teachers, not my mom and certainly not my last girlfriend, Linda Hawkins. She had told me she needed a man with a future, not some unemployed boy going nowhere. That was the moment I knew my future was ending there. I had to do something.

I had started seeing glimpses of the war in Vietnam on the TV in the front room, and I began to think that maybe it was a way out. God knows I'd never have enough money to leave otherwise. I had looked for a job, but pumping gas or working as a slave in a coal mine were not options I wanted to consider. Many of my buddies were in the same boat and were now talking about enlisting in the Army or the Marines and killing some "slopes" in the 'Nam, but it was mostly just talk. For me, the Army sounded like an adventure waiting to happen somewhere other than "Pennsylfuckingvania." Just how bad could Vietnam be, I had wondered? At least I'd have a regular paycheck, and maybe then I would get the respect I wanted and deserved, let alone the women. The women would be good. Women love a man in uniform, looking sharp. I would show them all, especially Linda Hawkins. And it was going to be warm, not shit ass cold and snowing like it would be if I stayed.

The heat and humidity of Vietnam soon became like home to me. "Ain't no big thang," I reminisced. It had been good to be a "grunt," an infantryman, but that had been a long, long time ago. Names and faces passed through my thoughts, some crystalline clear, others vague and watered down by time. Some of those memories filled me with anguish, while others were mixed with a sense of satisfaction, accomplishment, and brotherhood. My thoughts drifted again and I recalled another green, warm place…Hawaii.

Hawaii had sounded really good to me. If hula girls, palm trees, and surfing blue water in front of white sand beaches were included, how could I go wrong?

I had just finished AIT (Advanced Infantry Training) at Ft. Benning, Georgia so I knew as a "grunt" I was on the fast track to Vietnam. I was lean and hard from training and felt I was a real kick ass infantryman. As my first duty station since training, Schofield Barracks, Hawaii seemed pretty luxurious and exotic compared to the wooden barracks and drill sergeants of Fort Benning, Georgia. My only exposure to Hawaii prior to landing in Honolulu was from the Elvis movie "Blue Hawaii."

I had ended up in the Army just out of high school in 1965. As an eighteen-year-old, 135 pound, brown-haired, 5'6" country boy who grew up in small towns in Kentucky and Pennsylvania, I didn't know much about the world. I was about as raw as they came. With my infantry "buzz cut" hair, I looked like I was fourteen again. Truth be told, I hadn't really started shaving, except for swiping at the few hairs on my chin and a stray mustache hair here and there.

As I thought about how I came to be in the Army, I remembered that although I had no real work prospects after school, I wasn't the dumbest kid on the block. In high school I was a slacker, but I still pulled easy B's. I just needed something important to do. After some long talks in the kitchen, I convinced my mom that it was the right decision for me to join up, but my sister was worried. She cried when I left.

My vision of Hawaii as a paradise changed shortly after my arrival in mid-July 1966. When I landed at the Honolulu airport, I was unprepared for the beauty and smells of that tropical isle. I also had never seen so many Asian people in one place. Soul brothers I knew. I grew up and went to school with plenty of Negro kids and never had a problem or worry. When I went through Basic Training and AIT at Ft. Benning, my best friend was Roosevelt Clay. Roosevelt was eighteen just like me, but while I was skinny and short, he was 5'10", weighed 200 pounds and had a broad, round face, a large mouth with shiny white teeth, and a pudgy flat nose with big nostrils. A big, strong, dark-skinned Negro kid, he always seemed to have a smile and a positive outlook on life.

Roosevelt was also a damn good soldier and he felt just like I did, "Van, you and me are gettin' to fight the VC and NVA, and here we are in Hawaii with friendly folks who look just like them. I'm sure glad you're from Kentucky and talk with that slow talk of your people. I won't have no trouble keepin' you separated, you with your bald head and skinny white ass." Roosevelt was laughing deeply, as he usually did.

I was laughing, too. It was true, I thought. It was going to be tough to identify the good from the bad in Vietnam, and we were going to be on the ground right in front of both types. It was our job. We had all heard about how crafty the VC could be at blending in; it was on TV every night. We watched the war every chance we had, because we knew it soon would be us doing the fighting, not just watching it on the tube.

"You're right, my man. And let's face it, nobody is gonna mistake you for a VC, Roosevelt. They just don't make people that big over there. Besides, I think those boys know better than to fuck with us. We are ground pounding, ass kickin' grunts, man," I said, growling at Clay with my best tough guy face as I tried not to laugh.

Roosevelt and I were "grunts," officially riflemen, 11B10's in the 1st Battalion, 20th Infantry. The unit had just been activated at Schofield Barracks, Hawaii. The battalion was assigned to the 11th Infantry Brigade. Everyone knew why all new 11B10's were being assigned to Hawaii. It was the logical "jumping off" spot for Vietnam. Schofield Barracks was now empty, as it had just witnessed the departure of the 25th Infantry, the Tropical Lightning Division. That's why we were here. And the changes didn't stop there.

In August 1966, the 11th Brigade was reorganized into a Light Infantry Brigade configuration. The addition of a Delta and Echo Company to each infantry battalion went into effect shortly thereafter. Although a stiff challenge to all concerned, the transition from a four to a six-company battalion was made with little difficulty. As a private, I had little to say about anything as I shuffled from company to company, from squad to squad, and then again. Luckily,

Roosevelt moved right along with me, just like we were attached at the hip.

The reorganization also meant several armor officers in the battalion and brigade were now needed as infantry platoon leaders. Delta's newest LT was 1st Lieutenant Mike McDonald-Low, a 1208, armor officer. A tall, dark-haired, lanky, twenty-year-old from Oregon, Lt. McDonald-Low transferred from Charley to Delta Company in April 1967 and became my platoon leader. Also coming from Charley Company was Spec. 4 Michael Gates and Pvt. Immanuel Porter, both assigned to my squad.

As infantrymen in Delta Company, we soon learned that 100% of our time was to be spent in hard training and preparation for deployment to the Republic of Vietnam. Infantry companies like ours were soon spending nine out of every fourteen days in the field. "In the field" meant carrying sixty plus pounds of equipment on your back with a weapon in your hand, humping through the wet, muddy jungles of Hawaii's Koolau Mountains. I didn't weigh much to begin with and the shit I carried kicked my ass everyday.

There were some grunts who seemed totally oblivious to the load and the jungle at its rainy worst. Todd Lockhart was built like a gorilla and was the biggest guy in my squad and in the platoon. Todd was nineteen, blonde-haired, with boyish good looks and was 6'5" and 225 pounds of muscle. A good 'ol boy from Texas, Lockhart had a slow drawl and always ended every sentence with "boy" unless he was dealing with the LT or sergeants. Todd didn't say much, and I never saw him angry or heard him say a mean word about anybody, which was a good thing. He was just too damn big to have a chip on his shoulder.

Todd explained his view of infantry life to me one afternoon when we had stopped for a break on the side of a stream in the mountains. "This is no big deal, boy. Hell, I worked harder on my daddy's farm. Y'all don't want to have to bale hay from six in the mornin' to five at night in 100 degree heat. This is a cakewalk. We hump, it rains. We climb, it rains harder. We camp, it rains and the mosquito's come out. Here's the important thing, boy; ain't nobody shootin' anything at us but blanks. The only thing we ain't doing right now is fishin'. Thank yer lucky stars y'all ain't like Macintyre. That radio would kick yer ass, boy."

Radio Telephone Operator's (RTO's) carried all of their regular gear and ammo, plus a twenty-three and a half pound PRC-25 radio strapped to their back with two or three additional four-pound batteries in their rucksack. The PRC-25 was commonly referred to as "Prick 25" due to its weight. Radiomen spent their days with officers and platoon sergeants and were carefully chosen for the job. An experienced radioman became like a "private secretary" to the officer, anticipating what might be wanted and preparing it in advance. At night, he and the platoon leader, the platoon sergeant, and platoon medic had positions close together, alternating radio watch. The radioman also had to be able to understand and occasionally read maps. If the LT was engaged and moving, or if he was separated by circumstance, the RTO would be relaying commands, calling for medevac, and talking to the company commander.

Our platoon radioman, Pat Macintyre was a peach-fuzzed, twenty-year-old college kid from Lakewood, Washington. Mac had joined the Army after flunking out by partying too much at Central Washington State College. He was rawboned, broad shouldered and had close-cropped brown hair, and at 6'1" and 180 pounds he could carry that "Prick 25" all day. An ex-high school football player, Mac had a distinctive broken nose that complemented his toughness.

He had previously told me that when he was at Fort Polk for basic training, he was the only one that maxed the final P.T. test. I had already seen that he was good in the field. I never saw anyone who could low crawl as fast as him, even with the radio strapped to his back. It was like watching a snake slither through the jungle.

I asked Macintyre one day, when I saw him sitting alone, "Mac, how is it humping that beast all day? You run after the LT night and day while you nursemaid that radio."

Macintyre smiled at me and said in that long-winded college boy style of his, "Van Artsdalen, this job admittedly is not for everyone, but for me it's actually pretty cool. I like knowing what's going on and in this job I hear everything. The LT is pretty easy going so it's not that difficult. The weight and extra bulk of the '25' is a bitch and the batteries are no fun, but that's just part of the job. The best part is I get no KP or other shit jobs because the LT wants me available 24/7. I think I'm pretty lucky all in all."

I was a lucky one, too. All I had was my lightweight M79 grenade launcher, .45 caliber pistol, ammo, water, and my rucksack. I loved my M79; it was like a sawed-off shotgun with its 14"-long barrel. Unlike a shotgun, the single, 40mm barrel of the M79 was three times bigger; it was 1.6" in diameter, the shells were almost four inches long and weighed about one half pound. My M79 could send a high explosive grenade to a target up to 350 yards all day long. Its stubby fiberglass stock had no recoil, no kick. You squeezed the trigger and it made this hollow "thunk" sound. It was also great at up close and personal contact when I used my buckshot rounds, and that's what I planned to use when on patrol in the 'Nam.

Joining Roosevelt and Todd Lockhart in my squad was Alex Cerutti, a twenty-one-year-old Italian kid from New York. Dark-haired with bushy, black eyebrows and a hawkish face pockmarked from acne, Al was a smart ass and always had something to say about everything. He was also willing to defend his point of view because he was a fighter, and at 5'11" and 180 pounds, he was built for it. Tough as nails and a horrible slob, Al hated barracks life and was always in hot water with Sgt. Johnson, our squad leader.

"I think that son of a bitch is after me. He don't give me no respect, no matter how hard I try. He just busted my ass again and now I got KP. This ain't no life for an infantryman. This is not what I signed up for and look what I have now. I am a field soldier and a bad ass, gun-toting mother fuckah. I am not a fuckin' mess hall slave. I hate this shit in Hawaii," Cerutti ranted to no one in general. He then sat on his bunk and began polishing a brass belt buckle with a rag freshly dipped in Brasso.

I just laughed. Roosevelt did, too. "That fuckin' Cerutti, man. He bettah watch his ass with Sergeant Johnson 'cause the shit will hit the fan with that asshole. When we're here in barracks, that mother fucker will put him on KP for life, maybe even in the 'Nam," commented Clay in that slow southern style of his, smiling the whole time.

Bobby Zapata, a wiry, short, well-muscled Mexican kid from South Central LA was another one of our squad's teenage loud mouths and was also hot about Johnson, "Cerutti's right. That Johnson is all about fucking bullshit, man. He likes it here in barracks where everything is left, right, left, and if you fuck up, it's KP for you. He's all spit and polish. In the bush, it'll be a different story, man. They'll be no shit there, homey."

"At ease, men." It was Sgt. Gates and he appeared out of nowhere as Zapata was bitching.

He looked at each of us and said, "This is no time to be wasting your time, men. We are heading back to the Kahuka's tomorrow morning and we all have things to do. Let's get to it!"

Gates then turned his attention to Zapata, "Zapata, thank your "lucky" tattoo that Sergeant Johnson didn't hear you. Your shit talk will get you into nothing but trouble with that man. Do not, I repeat, do not fuck with him. It's not worth your time and it's definitely above your rank."

Michael Gates was twenty-four and one of the older grunts in our squad having spent several years in college before dropping out and joining the Army. He had been stationed at Ft. Polk, Louisiana, and hated it so much that he volunteered for the 11th Brigade and Vietnam. He had also just been promoted to sergeant and was our fire team leader and second in command to Sgt. Johnson in the squad. I liked him. He reminded me of my older brother whom I hardly knew, but he didn't look anything like him. Gates was blonde-haired, blue-eyed, six feet tall, had a medium build, and was from Southern California. He had "surfer boy" written all over him. The only thing he was lacking was longer hair and a better tan. His good looks and easygoing demeanor belied his total commitment to being a great soldier and making us better as well. He was not like Sgt. Johnson.

Emile C. Johnson was a Korean War veteran and enjoyed throwing his weight around in the barracks. He was slightly built at 5'8" and was somewhat prematurely balding. A Negro from the Midwest, he had been in the Army sixteen years and was still a Staff Sergeant, E-6. He boasted that he was ready for Vietnam and could hardly wait to "kick some VC ass." A real spit-and-polish NCO (Non Commissioned Officer) he was usually more concerned about our uniforms, boots, and how clean our barracks were than how we performed in the field. This bothered us because his field skills seemed lacking. When officers or other senior NCOs were around, he was all bluster and bullshit pointing out "our" mistakes and how he was working hard to turn us into better soldiers. Truth was, the mistakes were sometimes his, although he acted as if he knew everything about being a grunt. I wondered how Sgt. Johnson would react when the shit hit the fan in Vietnam. So did everyone else.

Chapter 4

BORN IN THE USA

Narrative: *Spec. 4 Clifford Van Artsdalen*
1966-67

Roosevelt, Todd Lockhart and I got along like "hot dogs and beer at a ball park," is what Sgt. Gates had said. Life was good for us because it meant it was simple. Not for some, but for us it was a breeze. While Todd and I had both grown up outdoors, Roosevelt was comfortable in the streets and in reading situations. The fact was, we were a great team and all three of us loved being in the field because, at least for now, the rounds we were constantly popping at each other were all blanks. It wasn't much different from playing hide and seek as a kid, except here you couldn't go home if you felt tired, hungry, or hurt.

Sgt. Gates also helped make it easy for us. He took us under his wing and I never saw the guy bat an eye when it came to making the right decision. He had a natural flair for leadership and he was solid in the field.

Lockhart and I made rank pretty quickly, jumping to Specialist 4 in just five months, while Roosevelt and Cerutti were stuck at PFC, largely because Cerutti couldn't keep his mouth shut in the barracks around Sgt. Johnson, and Roosevelt was just plain sloppy. But that was just in the beginning. Soon we were spending most of our time in the jungles of Hawaii.

I felt most at home in the rich vegetation of the Koolau Mountains on the North Shore of Oahu. We called them the Kahuka's, the name given to them by the locals. My platoon sergeant, Sergeant First Class Donald Hodges, recognized the way our squad easily negotiated through the bush and in steep, muddy terrain. Hodges wasn't easy to please. At thirty-six he was the oldest and most experienced of our NCO's, except for First Sergeant Taylor. A tough, hard-as-nails individual with no love for slackers, Sgt. Hodges didn't take any bullshit and nobody ever messed with him. Originally from Nebraska, Hodges had an easygoing attitude unless you screwed up. If he was in your face, you paid attention. The guy looked like he could eat a grizzly bear. A rangy, 180-pounder with close-cropped blonde hair, Hodges looked the part of platoon sergeant. He always seemed to have a two-day-old beard at three in the afternoon. It was unnerving when he stood close to you, as his blue eyes had a way of looking right through you.

Sgt. Hodges was not a "garrison" soldier, as he thrived in the field and in the real "business" of the Army. That doesn't mean he was easy in the barracks. He was focused on precision at all levels, but I never saw him bust anyone for not having their socks and underwear lined up properly in their footlocker. Weapons inspection was something else. He demanded excellence, and he was a perfectionist when it came to us maintaining our weapons. Just clean and operable was not good enough.

Sgt. Hodges was also Lt. McDonald-Low's right hand man, and for the twenty-year-old LT, it was a good thing. The LT was quickly learning the ropes of the infantry that summer and he relied upon Sgt. Hodges for advice. Hodges pointed out to the LT that he was going to need good "point men" in Vietnam, and 1st Squad had the best in the platoon. Led by Sgt. Gates, we had a "feel" for it and we were all soon spending much of our time leading the platoon. This was the easy part for me and it wasn't much different from hunting white tail deer at home. I had a natural way of finding the best way through difficult terrain.

A not so easy thing for me to adjust to was learning about eating and surviving exclusively on C-Rations. C-Rations consisted of a rectangular cardboard carton containing one small flat can, one large can, and two small cans. The big can was an "M" unit can (meat-based entree item), the two small cans were the "B" unit cans (bread items), and the "D" unit can was a dessert/fruit item. The small flat can usually had either cheese or cookie options. Everyone learned to carry and use a small "P38" can opener to open the cans. In the top of the box was a brown foil accessory pack and a plastic spoon wrapped in cellophane. The accessory pack had salt, pepper, sugar, instant coffee, non-dairy creamer, two pieces of candy-coated chewing gum, a small packet of toilet paper, a four-pack of cigarettes, and a book of twenty cardboard moisture-proof matches.

Each C-Ration carton had a packaged weight of 2.6 pounds. We tried to carry three or four days of C's when we were resupplied, so careful choosing and trading was a must to prevent adding the weight of unnecessary items. We heated the meals with cans of Sterno, but we knew in Vietnam it would be C4, plastic explosive. We had already seen the demonstration when we went through the Jungle Warfare Center. A quarter-sized piece of C4 could heat any C-Ration can to the point of boiling, and it did it fast and safe.

Cerutti loved C-Rations. He was also a master trader. While most of us in the beginning were content to stick with what we were given, Al soon taught us the ins and outs of negotiation, and it was a skill we honed for Vietnam.

"It's really easy. You just have to know the market you're dealin' with. It's basically understanding who eats what and who needs what you got. I know Roosevelt won't eat nothin' but chicken, beef stew, and peaches. I trade my beef stew for his cigarettes and then I trade those smokes to Nichols in 2nd Squad for a can of beanie weenies and a dessert. So I end up with what I want, and then some. Everybody's happy."

We were even happier when our field training came to a close. For me and the other grunts of Delta Company, our sixteen months in Hawaii had been a never-ending series of muddy, hot, rainy and mosquito infested humps into the Kahuka's. The Vietnam-like terrain of beautiful Hawaii with its endless mountains, valleys, streams and gullies challenged us at every turn. The many mock battles that the platoons and companies fought finally concluded when preparations for loading and shipping our gear to Vietnam began in earnest in the latter part of 1967. Our Kahuka days were over at long last.

Our uniforms and boots also changed at that time, when we were issued our tropical combat jacket, trousers and jungle boots for Vietnam. The new uniforms were a big hit with us because they were lightweight and had lots of big pockets. The jackets were worn outside the pant and we no longer had to worry about starching or ironing them. The new lighter weight jungle boots were also a welcome relief. Compared to the leather boots we wore during most of our training, the new jungle boots had a stronger, lugged bottom for better traction, were cooler, and they didn't retain water. We also didn't have to polish the whole boot, which was a big change. Just the toe and heel had leather to be polished and only during our last days in Hawaii.

Roosevelt liked the new uniforms and boots best. "Just look at this shit, man. These are cool with their baggy fit, big pockets and the way the jacket isn't tucked in. And the boots are like slippahs compared to those leather mofo's we was wearin'. I'll be a style setter in the Nam. Nuff of this Hawaii shit. We goin' to the big show."

Roosevelt was right. The new uniforms and boots put a period on our training in the mountains and jungles of Hawaii. We felt that we were finally ready, but if there were two things we were ignorant of as we completed our training in Hawaii, it would be of "Sir Charles" aka the Viet Cong, and his warlords the NVA, North Vietnamese Army. We weren't told much about our enemy other than he was tough, but not very sophisticated in his tactics. To us it didn't really matter. We were going to kick their ass. We didn't know it at the time, but we had a lot to learn.

Chapter 5

DESTINED TO BE A DOG

Narrative: *Lt. McDonald-Low*

1967

It felt good to leave Hawaii behind. There had been too many days filled with rain and mosquitoes on long humps in the red mud of the Kahuka's. Chasing what? After a while, it became a joke among most of us young LT's. And we were young. I was just twenty, a First Lieutenant, and a graduate of Officer Candidate School at Ft. Knox, Kentucky.

I was destined to be in the Army. My stepfather was an Army First Sergeant, an E8, when I had graduated high school. First Sergeant David G. Low was a World War II and Korea veteran, an infantryman since "Christ was a Corporal," as he liked to say. He was built out of bricks, graying at the temples, and could give you a look that would freeze you in your tracks. He had given me one month for raising hell after graduation, and then we had our "talk." It was July 1965, and we were standing in the kitchen. My Dad still had on his starched fatigues having just gotten off duty from Ft. Lewis, Washington, and he looked all business, as usual.

"I hope you had a good time with your buddies. It's now time we made a decision about your future," he said in that gravelly first sergeant voice of his.

I didn't like the sound of where this was going.

"The way I see it son, you've got a few things going poorly for yourself. Number one is instead of using that big brain of yours to get a college scholarship you decided to hang out with your buddies, ski, surf and chase pussy. You were good at some of those, but they will not be paying your bills or getting you into college. Second thing, instead of you using your time wisely over the past thirty days to find a job or some other worthwhile pursuit, you elected to go surfing. I warned you about being self-sufficient."

I knew better than to try to bullshit the old man. I had tried in the past, but it had always ended poorly for me.

"Before you respond, let me continue," he said. "On the other side of the coin, you've got some very good things going for you. You do have that big brain, you're tall and athletic, you're eighteen, and you know about the Army. I think it's time for you to enlist and then go to OCS to become an officer. But let's talk about that, too."

He had paused and then looked carefully at me, "You know Vietnam is happening and you know I'm going soon. If you're in the Army you'll be going as well. Now, let me ask you a question. When you have kids and they ask you what you did in the war, do you want to tell them you were a supply clerk, commo specialist, or some desk jockey?"

I shook my head.

"No, I didn't think so. You want to tell them you were an officer who led men into combat. So, you're either going to become an infantry, armor, or artillery officer. What sounds like your deal?"

This was no time for indecision, because I knew the old man wouldn't tolerate it. "I think I like the sound of tanks, 'cause I'm not keen on walking, or dragging some big ass cannon."

The die was cast. In August I joined the Army and by January 1966 I was at Ft. Knox for six months of hell and training at Officer Candidate School.

On 18 July 1966, I was commissioned a Second Lieutenant and I was assigned to Schofield Barracks, Hawaii, and the 11th Infantry Brigade. I was to be an armored cavalry platoon leader and I was stoked. It didn't last long. My armor days ended a few months later and before I could blink, I spent most of 1967 as an infantry officer. I'm sure my Dad was delighted.

The sixteen months of Hawaii jungle training had gradually molded our infantry units into tight knit cliques of fire teams, squads, and platoons who knew they were training for war in the big green of Vietnam. Our lot was mainly a mix of draftees, had-to-join-or-go-to-jail hard cases, and young volunteers eager to prove themselves. The racial tension of the late 60s existed as a subtle undercurrent in our company, but for our soldiers it rarely was an issue. We had a true cross section of America: Midwest farm boys, East Coast and Southern whites and Negroes, Puerto Ricans, Mexicans, Northern college boys and West Coast hippies; average age of about nineteen.

The mix of races and cultures helped blend and homogenize our platoons and company even further, though they all still maintained their own roots and core buddies. The harsh conditions of training also helped to gradually eliminate our troops' differences and focus them upon the enemy, which would change abruptly from the US Army, to LBJ, to the Viet Cong and NVA, and to the hippies in the States.

We thought we were ready. I was ready. In retrospect, we were physically prepared, but not mentally.

On 7 December 1967, at about 1600 hours, I and every other grunt of the 11th Light Infantry Brigade boarded the USS Gordon and USS Weigel, and we shipped out to the Republic of Vietnam.

UNACCOUNTED

On board ship, it was good to be an officer, even if I was just a 1st Lieutenant. As officers, we lived like princes in the domain of the U.S. Navy. I shared a stateroom with my three fellow Delta platoon leaders, 1st Lieutenants Jerry Swan and John Seifert, and 2nd Lt. Clarence "Fast Eddy" Robbin.

Jerry Swan was a skinny, tall, 6'4" crew-cut kid from Washington State. He was blonde, had an angular face, and a pronounced Adam's apple. A recent graduate of the University of Washington ROTC, he was twenty-two and had a mild manner and an easygoing way.

Seifert was from Philadelphia and was one of those guys who had a skeptical East Coast attitude about everything. John was twenty-three and a Ft. Benning Officer Candidate School graduate. He was 5'10", 175 pounds, brown-haired, handsome, and considered himself a real ladies man, like his counterpart from the "Big Apple," Clarence Robbin.

Robbin, who had just completed OCS at Ft. Benning, Georgia, was from New York, and was the newest and youngest LT in our group. As a nineteen-year-old Negro LT, he was one-of-a-kind. Handsome and light skinned, Robbin was short at 5'9", quick witted, a jokester and always had something smart to say. He liked us to call him "Fast Eddy" because as he told it, "Nobody is faster with the ladies than me!" Robbin was one of those guys everyone liked.

As officers aboard a U.S. Navy ship, our days were generally spent in full relaxation. We took our meals in the Officer's Mess along with all the other officers, including the captain of the ship and his staff. Waiters wore white jackets and pants and served us with white gloves. Our tables were set with linen and fine silverware. The glasses were plain, but glistening clean. The food was comparable to a better restaurant, though it used the same common ingredients the troops had in their mess.

After eating, we would confer with our platoon sergeants and check the day's activities for the troops and their well being. The rest of the morning we would spend relaxing and reading in the Officer's Day Room, or playing cards in our stateroom. We were not as bothered by seasickness as our troops because our quarters were higher in the ship where the air was clean and relatively odorless. It still smelled like an old ship with its aromas of iron, salt, and diesel, but we weren't consumed by them.

Our evening card games gave each of us a chance to learn more about one another and to bullshit, boast, and relate points of view on random subjects like women, combat tactics, dumb ass GI movies, and what we expected in Vietnam.

Seifert, ever the realist was unhappy one night, "Just deal the cards, Robbin. Enough talk about your platoon's superior fire and movement skills. That was Hawaii. Vietnam will be different. That gung ho Ft. Benning attitude of 'Follow Me' will get your ass blown off. Now, deal."

"No shit, Robbin. As the lowest ranking and only 2nd LT here, you best pay attention to your superior officers," I said laughing.

Jerry Swan wasn't far behind, "Look, I want to play cards. I don't want to be subjected to Mr. Robbin's tirade on his skills as a leader. Eddy, deal the cards."

Robbin shuffled the cards again, started dealing and as he did, he looked right at Seifert and said, "See what you've started. I tell you what Seifert. You know I'm a gamblin' man." Robbin looked at each of us. He then stood up, pulled a $100 bill from his wallet, and laid it on the table. He smiled and said, "Now let's play some cards, Sirs."

We all laughed and told him "fuck you very much" for his appreciation of our superior rank. Swan, as he shuffled the cards and laughed, said good-naturedly, "I don't know about you guys, but I've been thinking about a combat name for our company and I don't think we should have one." Swan paused, looked at everyone and then very seriously said, "Unless it was something like Delta Dawgs."

Seifert looked up from his cards and cracked up. I joined him. Robbin didn't get it.

"What he means, Lieutenant Robbin, is he wouldn't mind if we used the term 'Dawgs' as in the same name of the mascot at his fucking college. They were the Huskies, but more commonly referred to as the 'Dawgs.' Spelled D-A-W-G-S," Seifert explained to Robbins in that mock professor Philly accent of his.

At that moment, Swan said, "Call."

Each of us knew this was trouble. Swan never called a hand unless he had a sure winner.

"I don't see what the problem is. I didn't say Huskies, I said 'Dawgs.' It just seems right to me. Think about it. When you get right down to it, we'll be just like dogs in Vietnam. Always on the scent and prowl. And we're going to be treated like dogs: sleeping and eating outside, moving when we're told, fighting at our master's command. We are just 'Dawgs'."

We all liked it. And it was true. We were destined to be dogs.

Chapter 6

HELL ON THE HIGH SEAS

Narrative: *Spec. 4 Clifford Van Artsdalen*
December 1967

We all sighed with relief when we saw the rocky coastline of South Central Vietnam. Life aboard ship had been hell for me and the other enlisted grunts of the 11th Brigade. I had never been on anything larger than a ten-foot rubber raft, and the USS General W. H. Gordon troop transport ship was huge at 622 feet long and seventy-five feet wide. She could cruise all day and night at fifteen to twenty miles per hour, making our 6,000 mile trip to the Republic of Vietnam almost three weeks in the making. She had a crew of over 500, but it was hard to notice because we didn't just relax and stroll around. The 3,500 "guests" of which I was just one, another enlisted man, did most of the work. There were chores to do and meals to prepare. KP, latrine duty, and cleaning decks and holds on a troop transport ship was a 24/7 process.

Nighttime in the sleeping quarters was the worst time on board the Gordon. Located deep in the hold of the ship, myself and 3,500 other lower ranking men were below decks, stacked six deep in swinging hammocks. And swing they did, particularly when the weather was poor. Your gear was all around you and so was everyone else's. The troop hold smelled like a mix of diesel fuel, sweat, vomit, and saltwater. The closeness was penetrating. At night, when everyone was relatively quiet, you could still hear a dull cacophony of farts, coughs, sneezes, and puking.

One guy heaving would set the entire room off. If one guy puked, before you knew it, ten other GI's would start heaving, too. It really didn't matter where you came from or if you were white or colored. Seasickness was rampant on board the ship, especially the first week and during a three-day storm we experienced in the second week. The only one that seemed immune was Cerutti, and he had never been on a boat before. You could either ignore it and hunker down into your hammock or head for the latrine. I hunkered. I had no choice.

Deck time was only allowed for lower ranking enlisted men during daylight hours unless you were on guard duty or fire watch. The senior NCOs and officers of the company could go almost anywhere at anytime. The only time I saw Lt. McDonald-Low was when we were having weapon inspections, tactic instructions or PT. He had it easy along with the other LT's of Delta, and I'm sure he was never seasick. I rarely saw him in the morning; there was no wake-up call for the LT's.

Macintyre, the LTs' RTO confirmed my suspicions one day when I caught him coming back from a brief discussion with the LT who had just come on deck.

"Mac, what's going on with the LT? He looks pretty fresh with his starched jungle fatigues and sunburn."

"You do not know the half of it, Van Artsdalen. Those guys are living the life of leisure. Their uniforms are done for them; boots, too. They spend a lot of time out on the upper decks or hanging out in the Officer's Day Room. Guys serve their meals to them in white jackets and gloves. They hope it takes another month before we get there."

Mac seemed very delighted in telling me this info. His broad smile told me he was enjoying something about the LT's on-board lifestyle.

"I'm not lying, Van. The only things they don't have are women and TV. If they did, they'd probably seize command of the boat. What a life it is to be an LT."

It wasn't the same for the men of 1st Platoon or me. We began with reveille at 0515 with Sgt. Hodges kicking our ass out of our hammocks. Chow call for breakfast began promptly at 0600 hours and it normally took about forty minutes in line followed by five minutes of eating. Supper started at 1200 hours and the evening dinner bell was at 1730 hours. There was only so much space on deck and in the galleys, so we ate in shifts and had our deck time staggered. Our lives were pretty boring compared to barracks life and training back in Hawaii. After the first two weeks, we had all settled into life on-board and it had become tedious more than anything else.

On our last night at sea, Bobby Zapata, who had been sicker than anyone, said it best as the lights had just dimmed in the sleeping hold, "I don't know about you mother fuckers, but this fuckin' boat has just about killed my Mexican ass. I ain't ate for a week and my asshole feels like a truck been drivin' through. As weird as this sounds, I cannot fuckin' wait to get to Vietnam. Fuck this boat, man."

His declaration was greeted with a chorus of "Hell, yeah," "Fuck, yes," and "Dam straight!" No one would be reluctant to have his boots firmly planted on dry land, even if it was Vietnam.

As the USS Gordon began its docking maneuver, the first view that greeted us at Qui Nhon harbor was the battered hulks of two M48 main battle tanks that sat on the docks. Their hulls were pock marked with small arms' fire and they had their treads blown off. Next to them sat three armored personnel carriers that were also seriously damaged. Each was full of holes and just like Swiss cheese, some of the holes went all the way through. The buzz of our arrival was quickly replaced by a more solemn quiet. As we came off the Gordon, you could watch the men's expressions change from relief to concern when they spotted the heavily damaged armored vehicles. The message was clear. Vietnam was a war zone.

The "cowboys and Indians" phase of our training had truly ended.

Chapter 7

WELCOME TO THE SHOW

Narrative: *Lt. McDonald-Low*

December 1967

On 22 December 1967, the USS Gordon and USS Weigel, carrying the men of the 11th Light Infantry Brigade docked at the harbor of Qui Nhon, Republic of South Vietnam. We had arrived. When I walked off the Gordon to join the men of my platoon, I knew my days of easy living were over.

As platoon leaders, our first job after debarking was to get our platoons formed up and armed with their weapons and ammunition. While each soldier had carried his own weapon from Hawaii, they had been locked up other than for cleaning and inspections while on board. It would be the last time any of us would be separated from our weapons. This was also the first time the men had actually been armed with live ammo outside of the firing ranges of Hawaii. We gave the word to our platoon sergeants and squad leaders to instruct their men to load their magazines, but not to chamber any rounds. We wanted open breaches so there would be no accidents.

I was standing next to Captain Barry Marks, my company commander, and Lt. Jerry Swan who had just walked up to us with LTs Seifert and Robbin. Captain Marks was all business as he looked at us. His easy going Georgia accent was now clipped and direct, "Delta will be on the first load of trucks for the battalion. Have your men put their rucksacks into the last four trucks in the convoy: weapons, ammo and water only for the transport. I want you platoon leaders to have your platoon sergeants and squad leaders alert, but steady. Keep the men calm. We don't need any gunfire just because one your wild boys gets jumpy and thought he saw a VC. Stay in charge."

Marks paused and then said, "We don't expect any trouble on this transport and we will have plenty of help covering us for the trip. The truck convoy is escorted not only from the air, but once we start to move up Highway One you'll see an armored cavalry platoon join us as an escort. Their main battle tanks and armored personnel carriers have a lot of firepower so we'll be well armed. Let's get ready to load up and do our jobs. This is what we have all trained for."

Each of us saluted and as we walked away, I could feel the tension from that brief encounter with Captain Marks. To be honest, I felt a little wide-eyed. Everything looked, smelled and overwhelmed my senses. The surroundings all felt somewhat surreal to me, as I am sure it did to my fellow LTs. It was green and bright and beginning to warm at 1030 hours.

As I walked up and stood with Sgt. Hodges, I looked over the men of my platoon. They seemed nervous, especially when the dark green "Deuce and A Half's" (2 1/2 ton) trucks pulled up to transport us to LZ Carentan, eighty-eight miles north. Each truck carried about twelve men so we had a total of twenty, including the ones that carried our rucksacks and extra gear. Above the trucks, the six helicopter gunships that had followed them now circled lazily above us waiting for our loading and departure from the dock area. The gunships were to be our protectors for the trip and their deadly presence was a warning not to be ignored. The thwop-thwop of their blades provided a soon to be familiar backdrop for my first day "in-country" and it would become a sound that I would never forget.

The trip north averaged a speed of about fifteen miles per hour as soon as the armored cavalry joined us. The big M48 tanks could cruise faster, but the amount of dust generated by their tracks and the M113 APC's (Armored Personnel Carriers) at that speed was already blinding. All along Highway One we encountered small villages where the convoy would be forced to slow, allowing the dust to settle.

Local village kids, dressed in poor clothing, would assault each troop truck looking for candy bars and handouts.

While our troops were naturally drawn to want to give the kids treats, we had been forewarned to be on the alert; women and children were known to approach troop transport trucks begging for candy, only to then heave a grenade into the truck. We were trained to expect the VC to be everywhere and it made the trip nerve-wracking, a sure sign of things to come, and an indication of just how new we were to Vietnam.

Highway One followed the coast and we had glimpses of the China Sea as we rode along. To the west, I saw dark green mountains as they rose from the valleys and flat lands and extended beyond the horizon and borders of Laos. As I looked at the scenery rolling by, I thought about how Vietnam had been in a constant state of war since 1946, first with the French, and now with us. Hell, they had been at war longer than I had been alive.

I leaned over to Sgt. Hodges, pointed at the distant mountains looming to the northwest and said, "I would venture to say we will be spending most of our time out there. Looks like the Kahuka's."

"I believe you are absolutely goddamn correct, Lieutenant. We didn't spend sixteen months in the mountains of Hawaii to train these boys to fight the NVA in the flat lands.

Welcome to the beautiful countryside of Vietnam. You can bet your bottom dollar we'll be on the hump in those hills," Hodges said to me with a wan smile.

I looked around the truck, and nearly everyone was sweating through their jungle shirts, their faces wet and glistening under their helmets. After a month on the cool sea, Vietnam seemed sweltering though it was only about eighty degrees. Most of the talk was quiet, and many soldiers were just caught up in their own thoughts watching the scenery of a totally new and foreign countryside pass by. I listened to Gates, Clay, and Zapata as they absorbed their new surroundings.

"It looks a lot like Hawaii, probably about 300 years ago," Gates said, talking to no one specifically.

After a pause, Zapata was suddenly animated and with a deadly serious look on his face he waved his arm at the back of the truck, "You be right, Sarge. Look at the Nam, my brothers. Feels like Diego on a spring day. Ceptin' there are no cars, no paved highways, and no ladies in them short skirts. I am so fuckin' glad to be off that boat. Sarge, I tell ya I coulda' kissed the fuckin' ground when we landed. All I need me now is some pussy and I will be good to go to kick some NVA ass."

Everyone within earshot had a smile or was laughing outright. Clay was laughing hardest and when he could talk he said, "Zapata. You are a trip. The next thing y'all be asking for is a tent when we in the bush. Then you can axt the LT if we gonna get room service, too!"

At the mention of the word LT, everyone looked toward me, hoping I hadn't heard, but I had.

"Specialist Zapata. Specialist Clay. I do not believe there will be room service for us during our tour in the Republic of South Vietnam. I will pass your concerns on to Sergeant Hodges and have him confer with you both about it later," I said sternly, but with a subtle smile.

"Sorry, LT, I was just bull shittin' bout nothin'."

"At ease, Zapata. I was just checking your head space and timing."

Clay looked relieved. "Right on, LT. Gotcha," he said, all thumbs up with an eager smile.

Hodges just scowled at them. The talking ended.

Five hot, grueling, dusty, lung clogging, uneventful hours later, we arrived at our new home; LZ Carentan, Duc Pho, South Vietnam.

Chapter 8

AIN'T NO BIG THANG

Narrative: *Lt. McDonald-Low*
December 1967 – February 1968

If I thought our training in Hawaii was the end of our preparation for combat in Vietnam, I was wrong. For our first few days, including Christmas, we manned the bunker line and foxholes of LZ Carentan's northern perimeter. The following weeks we participated in training programs in search and destroy operations, ambush techniques, destruction of fortifications and food caches, helicopter orientation, and combat air assault familiarization. For our first month, we did little else but prepare to fight the enemy. During this time we also received our official radio call signs. Our company call sign was to be Crossbow Delta. I was Crossbow Delta Four Six, Robbin was One Six, Seifert was Two Six, and Swan was Three Six,. Cpt. Marks was Crossbow Delta Six.

One afternoon after returning to our bunker line, I watched my platoon medic, Nelson, passing out malaria tablets. He was talking to several soldiers as he gave each of them a large orange pill. "You must take these every day you sorry bastards. Malaria will kill you; if not here, later back in the world. And it isn't pretty. First, you'll get a high fever, anemia and severe flulike symptoms, such as shivering, joint pain and headaches. If not properly treated, it can lead to major organ failure and the big box. Trust me, you'd rather die from a gunshot than malaria. You better believe it."

Some grunts were invaluable to the men. It could have been the way they made everyone feel better. Or, it could have been that they were so solid and capable that they made everyone feel safer. Whatever it was, those men became a commodity. Something everyone wanted close by. Consequently, those men became so high in demand it made their lives in the field risky, as well as non-stop. Doc Nelson was our guy. He watched out for all of us, and some needed more care than others.

A few soldiers hid the fact that they did not take the malaria pills, preferring to catch malaria rather than remain in the field. Just another one of those crazy, horrible life choices some grunts made.

One day I asked Zapata, a rifleman in 1st Squad, when I saw him palm his malaria tab and put it in his pocket, "Zapata, what's up with you ditching your meds? Those orange pills will keep you from dying from malaria when you're back in the world. Haven't you listened to what Doc Nelson had to say?"

Zapata looked at me sheepishly and said very seriously, "LT, I'm like a cat. I got me nine lives, but I'm worried I'll be usin' some of those up with Sir Charles. I need to save me from the lead poisoning. If malaria come take my ass outta the field, I'll take it. Sorry about that, LT."

What could I say? I could bust him for not taking his meds, but then I'd lose a man that was good in the field. It was a losing proposition either way. Some things you have to let slide, and this was one of them for me.

As brave and foolish as Zapata was, he would never drink water from a stream or river in Vietnam without using his Halazone tablets. Halazone was supplied in small, brown, glass bottles. Two tablets dissolved in a one-quart canteen would disinfect the water, while passing along a strong smell of chlorine. It also didn't taste great, but it was better than the alternative.

Sgt. Hodges and I quickly decided we needed a checklist of supplies when we were headed to the jungle because we were both seeing too many personal and useless items being brought. Everything we carried was for day-to-day survival and it already weighed from sixty to eighty pounds, so eliminating unnecessary weight was a must.

The "Basic" Checklist:

- Helmet
- M16 and/or Weapon
- Bayonet
- 20 M16 magazines (or weapon equivalent, loaded, 20 rounds each) bandoliers
- 6 – 10 cardboard boxes of ammunition – 20 rounds each
- Rucksack with aluminum frame
- Pistol belt
- Ammo pouches (4)
- Field bandages (2)
- Morphine syrette
- Flashlight with 4 batteries
- Mosquito repellant
- Halazone salt and malaria tabs
- 4-6 hand grenades
- 3-4 days of C-Rations
- 2 smoke grenades
- 1 Claymore mine with hand igniter
- 1lb bar of C-4
- 4 - 1 qt. canteens of water
- Entrenching tool
- 3 pairs of socks, underwear, t-shirts
- Towel and toothbrush
- Poncho
- Poncho liner
- Personal effects – no cologne, hair gel, shave cream, deodorant, or anything with an odor.

Besides having the right gear, one of the biggest lessons we learned early in those training operations was about our most basic infantry weapon; M16s that didn't fire or jammed was an operator problem you didn't want to have. M16s had to be taken care of and cleaned and checked at every opportunity. Mud was a constant problem, generally treated by a good flushing with water from your canteen, then an oil rub down the barrel with a patch of tissue paper from your C's as a swab. It was also a good idea to keep the twenty round magazines clean, as they would clog and jam even faster.

It was also a bad idea to use your M16 as a pole to help a buddy up out a rice paddy or up an embankment. The weapons were loaded, and many grunts never had their weapons' safety engaged. The first person in our battalion to die in Vietnam was killed this way. The word spread like wildfire after it occurred and I never heard of it happening again. Simple, deadly lessons stick in your head.

Our training finally concluded in late January when we moved to our main battalion base camp at LZ Bronco to begin combat operations in the relatively quiet Duc Pho Area of Operations. It was also when we started regularly using helicopters as our primary means of transport in and out of Bronco.

We were all happier when we "rode" to work and we were now getting used to conducting frequent CAs - combat air assaults. We all quickly learned to love "Huey" helicopters.

UNACCOUNTED

The Bell UH-1D series Iroquois, better known as the "Huey," was our flying limousine on CAs. We called them "slicks" because they were mainly for transport and weren't armed with rockets and mini-guns like gunships. Each slick had a pilot, a co-pilot, and two door gunners manning M60 machine guns. One of the door gunners doubled as crew chief. Slicks could carry six infantry troops fully loaded into combat and more importantly, could haul those same troops out of tight spots. They also delivered our resupply of C-rations, ammo, water, and mail.

When we headed in or out of an LZ on a combat air assault it was always funny to me to see infantry troops sitting on their helmets. The first time I saw this was when we were unexpectedly put on alert and airlifted to LZ Leslie one afternoon. It was our first trip into the Que Son Valley.

Sgt. Hodges, Macintyre, and I boarded our slick with Clay, Porter, and Jackson who then calmly removed their helmets and sat on them. I looked at the three, "What are you men thinking?" I yelled at them above the air and rotor noise of the slick as it lifted off.

"Watcha mean, LT?" Clay shouted back.

"Why are you men sitting on your helmets?" I shouted.

The three looked at each other and then Porter with a broad smile on his dark face said to me, "LT, it's so we don't get our balls shot off. I still have 292 days and a wake up before I'm back in the world."

Everyone kept track of time in Vietnam, not by hours but by days left in country. Porter knew exactly how many days he had left in Vietnam and wasn't taking any chances. I couldn't believe it. They actually believed their steel pots would save their balls if a round penetrated the aluminum floor of the chopper.

I laughed to myself, smiled, and yelled at the three, "That should be the least of your worries, men. If a round comes through this hull, saving your balls will not be the issue. Hell, the whole aircraft is likely going down."

Clay, Porter, and Jackson looked again at each other and back at me. "Ain't no big thang, LT, least we'd have our balls," Clay yelled, and they each started smiling, laughing, and poking each other.

There was nothing more I could say. They were as happy as if they had each just received candy from home or a love letter. Mail Call was something we all eagerly awaited, especially in Vietnam. It wasn't uncommon for us to get a backlog of mail kicked out the door of a slick along with our three-day supply of ammo and Cs. Mail Call brought good news, bad news, girlfriend photos, snack food, underwear, and love letters. It was our only attachment to home, which we all called "Back in the World." "Back in the World" was not just the good ol' USA; it also referred to your city, your state, your neighborhood, your friends, and your goal of survival.

After listening to Clay's explanation about why he sat on his helmet, I thought of how my relationship with the men of my platoon had changed. A big rule we were taught at OCS was to keep the enlisted men we commanded at arm's length. This supposedly allowed us to be able to put men in harm's way without having to deal with the personal aspects of the man. It may have been the way the textbooks read, but when you're in the jungles of Vietnam day after day this rule does not apply in its strictest sense. You become more like "brothers" and you find yourself fighting harder to keep each other alive more than anything else. When I first came to Vietnam, I was fighting for my country, but the fight eventually boiled down to me doing my best for the men in my command, my brothers in arms. With this in mind, I could communicate as I did with those men, but I still expected my orders to be carried out implicitly. It was a good relationship and it was reflected in the simple pleasures we all shared.

As we circled LZ Leslie, Sgt. Hodges leaned over to me and said as he pointed at the firebase, "Take a good look at this place, Lieutenant. This is where truly bad things went down. The 1st Cavalry was overrun here, and look where the forces they faced came from; the NVA bull rushed straight down from those ridges. They then swept across those low hills like Grant went through Richmond. I'm guessing it was fifty to one down on the line. Brave cavalrymen died there. It was not pretty."

LZ Leslie was a small fire support base with sand bagged bunkers and concertina wire surrounding its perimeter. Situated on a small rise, Leslie was surrounded by small hills on three sides. On the fourth side was a ridge covered in lush vegetation that ran down to the floor of the valley across from the firebase. LZ Leslie was just large enough to be occupied by a single rifle company on the perimeter, a 105-artillery battery in the middle, and a four-barreled .50 caliber machine gun and searchlight crew for support. The landing zone had room for a single helicopter, and it was tight. Our lift of six slicks would be setting down just outside the perimeter where I now saw red smoke marking the LZ.

After we landed, Sgt. Hodges and I moved our troops through the opening in the concertina wire and then settled the men into their bunkers. As we moved from bunker to bunker, Sgt. Hodges told me how in the dead of night on 3 January 1968, just a few weeks before, units from the 2/12th, 1st Air Cavalry positioned at LZ Leslie and LZ Ross had been attacked simultaneously. Ross held, but Leslie was overrun.

I could see why. Leslie was a small, terrible place to defend and it had that war torn, dead-zone atmosphere to it. The bunkers on the perimeter were full of holes. In some places it looked as if someone had taken a shovel and stabbed at the sand bags, gouging and tearing them. The hills and ridge were so close they seemed to stare down at you, and it made the troops light-footed when they moved outside their bunkers. I don't believe anyone relaxed there. I think the men actually felt safer out in the bush than behind the concertina wire of Leslie.

I listened to Milner talking to Van Artsdalen about the firebase, "Van this place gives me the creeps. That bunker I'm in has bloodstains on the walls. Those boys in the Cav were in it up to their necks here. Look at this place. I feel like a trapped rat."

"Randall my man, you are absolutely right, but what can we do? We're here."

"This is fucking bullshit, Van. Leslie is a fucking dead man's location. Look at those hills. You know the dinks are thick in there. This ain't no firebase, it's a suicide location."

"Well then, buddy you should be happy. I've heard Weapons Platoon and a squad from 1st and 3rd Platoons will be going to an LZ named Charley Brown. We'll be leaving in the next day or two, while the rest of the company stays here."

On 30 January, my reinforced platoon was deployed to the small coastal firebase of LZ Charley Brown on the southern end of our AO. We had been sent to protect the small Navy base there, as well assisting the small contingent of ARVN troops protecting the adjacent fishing village of Sa Huynh. We already knew that it was an easy assignment with infrequent patrols occurring outside the base.

Charley Brown occupied the tip of a narrow, hilly peninsula that surrounded and overlooked a small island and bay, as well as Sa Huynh. On the outside of the peninsula was the China Sea. Between the peninsula's tip and the shores of San Huynh village was a distance of just 100 feet. On the inside of the peninsula was a small bay. In the middle of the bay was "Gilligan's Island," and it wasn't an island at all, it just looked like one. On Gilligan's was a small contingent of Navy personnel who operated four huge, wheeled, amphibious barges called BARCs. The BARCs had transported us across the narrow gap between Gilligan's and LZ Charley Brown, but their real mission was going around our peninsula and out to the China Sea to pick up military goods brought down by Navy cargo ships. The BARCs would then haul the cargo back to Gilligan's where they would be off-loaded onto trucks for transport to American bases north. Our job was to make sure nothing happened to them.

UNACCOUNTED

On our first afternoon, Sgt. Hodges and I were checking our bunker line on the side of the perimeter that overlooked the village. The village seemed very active, almost festive to me. Sgt. Hodges informed me that the next day was the lunar New Year in Vietnam and the official start of their Tet. I had never heard of Tet and figured it was no big deal, just another weird Vietnamese holiday. I was wrong.

That night and the next morning the North Vietnamese Army launched a series of surprise attacks on military and civilian locations throughout Vietnam. In the north, Hue, Danang, Chu Lai, and Tam Ky were all under assault by VC and NVA troops who had flooded out of the mountains of the Que Son. Our radios were ablaze with constant updates and reports of battles raging throughout the Americal Division AO.

At Charley Brown it was just another day, but we were on high alert because of the action to our north and south in the bigger cities. The bunkers were all manned and ready, the mortars were registered, but the only thing that happened was a few gunshots fired in mid-afternoon from the village, and they weren't directed at us. That night our three 81mm mortar's kept the LZ and village lit up with flares just to make sure everyone knew we were ready. The next four days for us passed without incident, but the battle for Hue and other cities had just begun.

Tet changed everything. It was the first time the NVA demonstrated their willingness to use a large number of troops in coordinated attacks and then commit them to holding and defending their gains. It shocked U.S. commanders throughout Vietnam. In the end, the North Vietnamese suffered massive casualties and were beaten back to their mountain bases, but they had made their point, at least politically; the war was not over and they weren't going anywhere.

Chapter 9

ANTENNAS KILL

Narrative: *Lt. McDonald-Low*

February 1968

After Tet, my command at Charley Brown was extended to five weeks. We wouldn't be rejoining the company until March.

On 5 February 1968, at 1000 hours, Delta Company humped out of the perimeter of LZ Leslie to conduct Search and Destroy operations. Mac and I were listening on the radio following their progress from Charley Brown.

"I'm sure everyone heaved a sigh of relief as they passed through the wire," I said to Mac.

"No, shit, LT. We all hate that place."

For the next few hours we listened as the company moved slowly from the close, low-lying brushy hills that surrounded the firebase, finally reaching small rice paddies set against the edges of the larger hills that led to the mountains and Laos. There were about twenty hooches spread out along the banks of the paddies.

The company was deployed in three staggered files with 2nd Platoon and HQ's in the center and 1st and 3rd Platoon's on either flank. As lead elements from 2nd Platoon crossed the paddy and reached the first hooch a sniper shot was reported fired.

Swan's 3rd Platoon had fanned out on the left bank and rushed the forward tree line, a distance of about fifty yards. There was no fire being directed at them as they ran towards the direction of the sniper. About a minute later, Swan reported that their search had turned up empty.

Mac and I then heard a nervous, excited voice call on the radio, "Delta One Six, Two Six, and Three Six, this is Delta Six Alpha. Delta Six is down, request your presence, over."

Our company commander, Captain Barry Marks had been shot.

I listened to his RTO on the radio requesting Dust Off from battalion.

I called Seifert. "Two Six this is Four Six, what's the situation? What do you know, John?" I asked.

"Jesus, Mike. We were moving, and one of his RTOs came up to him and wham! I saw him fall to the ground. What the fuck."

I couldn't believe it. We'd been shot at before, but no one had ever been hit. This was the first time.

"Christ, John. How could this happen?" I asked.

I then answered for him, "It was the radios wasn't it?"

I then heard in the background, Callahan, Six's RTO, saying, "When the shot was fired, Captain Marks had just gotten on the radio and the other RTOs were right behind us. Fucking lucky shot."

I didn't think so.

"Four Six, this is Two Six. Six doesn't look that bad. He isn't in any pain and he seems calm. The wound was just above his collarbone on his lower neck, and it appears to be through and through. It just doesn't look that serious. Here comes the Dust Off, I gotta go."

Thirty minutes later I heard that Marks had died, bleeding to death, just as he reached the forward field hospital at LZ Baldy. Captain Barry Marks, our Delta Six, had become the first casualty of Delta Company.

It was a heartbreak and loss to all of us. It shook me to the core. Barry was an officer everyone wanted to be like. A handsome, college educated Georgian, and already a Captain at age twenty-four, he was Brigadier General Andy Lipscomb's Aide-de-Camp in Hawaii. Lipscomb was the CG of the 11th at the time, and Marks, with his easy southern drawl was his right hand man. Marks could have gone to Vietnam as the General's Aide, but instead volunteered to take over Delta Company when the 11th Brigade was reformed into its light infantry configuration. Married with a child and a huge military future ahead, we all wondered what he was thinking when he chose to be the head grunt of Delta Company.

Later that afternoon, when Delta Company again received sniper fire from another small village to the north, I saw how frustration and loss quickly turned to anger and revenge. We listened as 3rd Platoon advanced on the small ville' comprised of about fifteen to twenty hooches that sat in a semi-circular pattern around a small pond.

"Three Six, Two Six, over."

"Three Six, go."

"Three Six, I see a plume of white smoke rising from somewhere at the end of the ville'. What's going on over there? You guys having a barbecue?"

"Negative Two Six. I had a trooper in my 3rd Squad decide to take things into his own hands to solve the problem with the snipers. The dumb ass set fire to one of the hooches and before we could do anything, the whole place started to go up. We're moving out. This was not a great public relation's statement for us. The villagers are fucking pissed. They're all yelling, screaming, and crying at us. We're leaving."

"Roger that. Not a good thing."

That night all of us platoon leaders held a radio meeting to talk about our situation and Marks' death. Swan said it best, "Look where we are at. This is the real deal in the Que Son. Antennas are like directional signals to snipers here and they always point to the officers who use them. Antennas will kill us."

Robbin, who took the loss of Marks the hardest of us all, said tearfully, "They killed our Six. The best CO I ever had and we did shit. We didn't even see the son of a bitch."

Seifert comforted Robbin in an unusual display of emotion, "It's okay, man. We got this. We've all been here since the beginning, like brothers. We have to move on. We learn from this and take comfort in the fact we will take those fuckers down for him."

"That's right, Ed. Listen to John. From now on we'll keep those fuckin' radios away from us," I added.

Each of us took the lesson to heart, as did our radiomen. From that day forward, we tried to keep our RTOs several men away from us when we were on the move. We were even more careful when we stopped to use them, and we tried never to be on them in the open. Among the troops, it became a black joke to see who would be the lucky one to "play" officer for the day and position themselves near the radios of the company.

Dying in Vietnam scared the hell out of everyone: captains, LTs, sergeants, and privates. No one wanted to die or be horribly maimed. The randomness, ferocity, and frequency of death in country helped bring real meaning to the slang expression "Ain't no big thang." It soon became our undeclared motto. No matter how terrible the circumstance, it would be far easier to handle and move on with that simple expression. It also helped us accept, embrace, and become indifferent to the suffering of our enemies as we brought terrible harm upon them. Ain't no big thang.

"Don't mean nothin'" was another riveting expression of infantrymen, and was used to dismiss witnessing or experiencing something so horrific that it couldn't be comprehended by the psyche. Alternately it was used as an expression of relief that one had avoided being killed, even if they were injured or maimed. It also developed into to an attitude with some grunts. For those few it was a permission slip to carry out the killing of enemy soldiers with absolutely no remorse or feelings. Don't mean nothin'.

"Sorry about that" was also a favored phrase I heard frequently, and it became the catch-all for truly dumb and terrible things that happened in the bush. Near misses from friendly fire were one of my favorites. Invariably in a firefight, when units are moving and attempting to stay engaged with the enemy, gunfire from a nearby platoon or platoon member would sometimes come too close. It never failed though that once things calmed down you heard the apologies. "Christ almighty, LT. Sorry about that. I didn't realize you guys were so close. I almost shot your ass off." Sorry about that.

No one ever spoke of the fire at the village.

Chapter 10

WHAT'S YOUR TWENTY?

Narrative: *Lt. McDonald-Low*

February – March 1968

While I continued to command LZ Charley Brown, our new Delta Six, Chuck Sonata, was spending his time with the other platoons on perimeter duty at LZ Bronco. He was familiarizing himself with the company and getting his feet on the ground.

It didn't take long for the word to spread amongst us LTs that our new company commander couldn't accurately read a map. Sonata had a clever way, however, to cover this issue in the field. He just called his platoon leaders for their location and then relayed that info to battalion or to artillery. He would do it even if he was within eyesight.

Knowing where you were in Vietnam was crucial, but sometimes map coordinates weren't enough. In the jungle it was difficult for the helicopters to identify our exact location until we "popped smoke." Smoke came in several colors: red, green, purple, and yellow.

As wonderful as smoke grenades could be to help you, they could also be a real pain in the ass. When our battalion commander, Lt. Colonel Edwin T. Beets wanted to "observe" his maneuvering companies on the ground, he would give orders to have the lead platoon of the company pop smoke so he could identify our forward position. This was awful for us, particularly if you were in the lead platoon, because we were actually trying to move stealthily without attracting attention to ourselves. Popping smoke not only told him where we were, but also any nearby NVA and VC.

Although Sonata couldn't read a map, Lt. Colonel Beets could, and to him distances and dangerous terrain didn't really matter. From 1,000 feet up in the air, a hill that is labeled 348 meters on the map appears to be a lot smaller when you look down upon it from altitude. If you are on the ground like we were, 348 meters is in fact 1,142 feet straight up the side of a slippery, muddy, dank, jungle infested, treacherous mountainside. It made no difference to him. I have heard him give orders to pursue three NVA located two grid squares away from us, heading away from our location. Two grid squares was 2,000 meters (6,650 feet) and in between that distance was another 1,500 meters (4,920 feet) of up and down terrain.

There were times we were thankful for the double and triple canopy cover so Budweiser Six couldn't spot us, or when we were at the extreme range of his time on station in his chopper. After a while we also learned to just say, "Six, I am going as fast as I can," or "I can't get there before dark." They didn't like us moving at night, unless it was to set up ambush patrols. We lost my good friend, 2nd Lt. "Fast Eddy" Robbin that way in early March near LZ Sue.

The company was drawn up into a night defensive perimeter, and it was Robbin's turn to send out an ambush patrol from his platoon at dusk. Shortly after 0300 hours in the morning he had lost radio contact with the patrol.

It was Macintyre's time at radio watch and he woke me when he heard about the trouble. We listened to the radio chatter and at 0430 hours we heard Budweiser Six order Delta Six to prepare for a combat air assault to a new location at first light, 0530 hours. When the "Big Six" was told One Six had lost contact with the ambush patrol, he was furious.

"Budweiser Six to Delta Six. I do not understand what your problem is. Get those men on recall immediately and get that company ready to go. I've got twelve birds arriving and I don't want any delays. Do you roger, over?"

"This is Delta Six, roger that."

Mac leaned over to me and said, "This is a bad fucking deal, LT. If Lt. Robbin has to go out there and retrieve that patrol in the dark, it will not be a good thing. Six can't be serious."

As I started to respond, I heard Captain Sonata calling Robbin on the radio, "One Six, retrieve your squad and do it immediately. We've got a lift to catch and we are not missing it. Now get moving!"

"Six, this is One Six. I am reluctant to approach a set ambush position at night. I have no radio contact. I request to wait until first light, over."

As I listened on the radio, I was thinking I would have been hard pressed to go as well. Sonata called again and told him, "Negative, One Six. Get your ass out there and get those men back in time for the lift. Six, out."

I didn't envy them. The night was partly cloudy so the moonlight was coming and going. I listened for the next five minutes staring at the radio. Sgt. Hodges who was listening with Mac and I said, "Lt. Robbin and his RTO should be using flares and flashlights to get the attention of that ambush before they get too close. If he's moving too quietly, they won't know it's him."

After a few minutes I heard the radio static, "Delta Six, Delta Six, this is Delta One Six Alpha, over." It was Quirk, Robbins' RTO.

"Delta Six, go."

"Delta Six, we have reached the ambush position and there is a problem. We need a Dust Off. Delta One Six is Kilo India Alpha, and I am Whisky India Alpha, over."

Kilo India Alpha, KIA, killed in action. Whisky India Alpha, WIA, wounded in action. The words rolled through my head. "Fast Eddy" Robbin was dead.

I heard later that as he approached the ambush site Robbin had called out, "Delta One Five," hoping not to surprise the squad.

It didn't work. At the sound of Robbins' call the squad set off their Claymore mines and went to full automatic fire. Thirty seconds later, their ceasefire and subsequent search revealed they had killed Lt. Robbin with the Claymore blast. His RTO, Bill Quirk, had miraculously been spared and suffered only a few fragmentation wounds to his arm and shoulder.

All of the LTs of Delta learned a serious lesson that dark morning. The men we were leading also learned something important . . . command was not a perfect science, and it was potentially deadly.

It also meant my time as Delta Four Six was over. I was going to be the new One Six and the Weapons Platoon was going to trade in their mortars for M60 machine guns and join the three rifle platoons of the company. The men from First and Third Platoons who had been with me at Charley Brown would be rejoining their respective platoons. The company needed them all as the attrition from non-combat injuries was proving to be a relentless problem in the company. It wasn't uncommon for there to be ten to fifteen men unavailable due to ankle sprains, jungle rot, lacerations or overall poor health. Vietnam was tough on grunts.

Chapter 11

SMOKE'EM IF YOU GOT'EM
Narrative: *Spec. 4 Clifford Van Artsdalen*
March 1968

Delta Company participated in numerous Search and Destroy operations through late March, and by then the Americal Division had renamed the missions "Search and Clear." I didn't think much of it either way. We were not doing anything different; our mission was to destroy the Viet Cong military forces in the Duc Pho District. During this time we made infrequent contact with the enemy, and when we did, it was usually initiated by Viet Cong in hit and run, guerrilla style attacks; they would spray us with automatic weapons or AKs and then disappear into the countryside. Their fire was rarely close, but it was close enough that it kept us on our toes and remembering where we were.

And forget about speed or stealthy movement. It would have been difficult for us to move seventy to 100 guys anywhere fast and quiet, even if we had them in their socks and underwear. Humping steep, overgrown, and muddy hillsides with seventy-plus pounds of gear on our back, humidity at 100% and the temps in the 90's also didn't help. Everyone lost weight. I heard the LT saying he went from 175 pounds to 155 pounds. I didn't have any body fat to begin with and I was now a slim, 130 pounds. Now in our fourth month, we were all gaunt and stripped to the bone of any excess weight. Our jungle fatigues hung on us and, being that we never washed or shaved in the field, we smelled and looked as if we lived dirt bag poor in the jungle.

Our squad had changed, too. We were now a heavy squad with our own M60 machine gun. In my squad there was squad leader Johnson, and fire team leaders Michael Gates and T. Smith. Bobby Zapata, Immanuel Porter, and Randall Milner were riflemen like Clay and Todd Lockhart. Jimmy Slatten and I were the M79 grenadiers. Our M60 crew included Cerutti as gunner with Bob Banks and Ronny Jackson who were grunts, as well as ammo bearers for Cerutti. All in all in the squad we had seven white guys, one Mexican and five Negroes. It didn't take long for everyone to learn there were few inequalities in the infantry, we were all just "grunts."

When we weren't patrolling, we'd either stand-down at base camp or we'd pull bridge security detail. Between Charley Brown, LZ Bronco, and points north, Highway One was the only route and it was used exclusively during daytime hours. All along the highway from its originations on the very southern tip of Vietnam to the northern DMZ, American units operated a series of bridge checkpoints. Bridges were vulnerable along the highway as they provided the VC and NVA a great location to seriously disrupt military supply traffic while inflicting casualties.

Despite the risk, we all loved bridge security work and there were always plenty of volunteers for the duty. The bridges we guarded were not really bridges at all as I knew them. They were typically just culverts running under a wooden bridge that connected the rice paddies from each side of the road. At each end of the bridge there was a heavily sand bagged bunker large enough for six men. Each bunker was positioned with an M60 machine gun in addition to their normal complement of M16s and M79 grenade launchers. Each bunker ran three men awake and three sleeping at each position, all night. Two hours on, two hours off. We had our Claymores out and at each end of the bridge we had concertina wire strung out blocking the highway. We took our jobs seriously, not so much because of our concern for the bridges, but because we were a good fifteen minutes out from any gunship help and nobody wanted to die for a bridge to nowhere.

The bridges along Highway One opened at daylight when we took our concertina wire down. During the daylight hours things were pretty slack with traffic passing freely. The emphasis for us was on rest, music, bullshit, smoking cigs, buying ice-cold Coke and rice treats from the "Coke Boys," and partying with their "Boom-Boom" girls. Although there was always a man up at each bunker on each end of the bridge looking official and watching, the rest of us were on easy street. Some men took their bridge security work too seriously, like Roosevelt. He had fallen in love the first time he laid eyes on "Marybelle," as he called her. He couldn't say her Vietnamese name, and to him it really didn't matter. He lost his virginity to that "Boom-Boom" girl, and I never saw him happier.

It was also during this time that helmet tattoos inked with pens and markers began to appear in the platoon and company. The graffiti worn by our grunts on the camouflage covers of their steel pots were varied and wrought with themes of death, bad attitude, and perverse humor. Cerutti wore "Kill'em All, Let God Sort'em Out"; Zapata's said "Shoot first, No questions"; and Macintyre, ever the collegiate had "Not a tourist, I live here" on one side, and "What about Napalm?" on the other. More of my favorites included "Warning: Being in Nam May Be Hazardous to Your Health"; "Day Tripper"; "Bad Mother Fucker, Made in Brooklyn, USA"; "Fuck This Place"; "Born to Die"; and not to be out done, Roosevelt proudly stenciled "Mommy, Can I

Go Out and Kill Tonight?" right on the front of his helmet. I kept it simple with mine: "Shit happens, then you Die," I thought captured it all. Sgt. Gates declared his mission with "Surf Vietnam." No surprise there.

Helmet graffiti was the one and only way we could express ourselves, and no senior NCO or officer ever gave us grief over it. Your "ink" was off limits to everyone except you, and this was especially true if you had been here long enough to earn your ink, as each of us was now doing.

FNGs or "Fuckin' New Guys" had no ink and they were easy to spot. An FNG was anybody who was new to the unit and had no combat or limited combat experience. An FNG was never trusted in a leadership role, regardless of rank, until they had been in the shit enough times and could be counted on to be responsible. It wasn't uncommon to see some squads run by E-4's when there might have been a sergeant within the squad, but he was an FNG.

I watched Sgt. Hodges check some FNGs the platoon had just received. "How did it go, Sergeant Hodges?" I asked when he had finished his inspection of the three new grunts.

"It never ceases to amaze me the absolutely crazy things these young troopers will attempt to carry, Van Artsdalen. Sleeping bags, gloves, flip-flops, comic books, baseball gloves, two pairs of boots, shampoo, shaving cream, and hair tonic is what I have just removed from their rucksacks," Hodges itemized with exasperation. "It was all stuff that weighed too much and replaced the things they really needed like ammo, water, and Cs, but they're squared away now and good to go."

"I'm sure they'll appreciate it later, Sarge," I replied still thinking about the "necessities" they had brought with them to the bush. I was glad he checked. I hated stopping because some fool had heat stroke from carrying too much crap.

When we were on the move as a company in the field, it was typically at a slow pace. Each platoon was usually working independently, but in contact with and sometimes overlapping other platoons. The very nature of Search and Clear was stop and go. If the stops were lengthy, or if it was time to take on water, "Smoke'em if you got'em," would ring out up and down the line by Sgt. Hodges and we would stop, drop our rucksacks, and assume hasty defensive positions facing outward.

I was always busy when we stopped because with our squad being in front, we didn't have the luxury of someone guarding our front. Sure I smoked, but just about everyone smoked. Smoking gave us all a measure of relief; it calmed and helped us focus better. I guess it was also that "one foot in the grave" outlook, and it was good to kill the hunger we all sometimes felt.

As I was my watching my front, Sgt. Gates came up, knelt down beside me and took off his helmet. "The LT and I have been up and down the line, and he wants you to go extra slow when we head out again. It's getting late and Doc Nelson is working with Porter's feet, but we are generally good to go."

Just then I heard a call coming from behind us, and I saw the LT with Macintyre and Sgt. Hodges passing Zapata and heading for us.

"LT, it's starting to get late. Have you heard what the plans are? What does Six have in mind?" I heard Sgt. Hodges ask the LT.

Mac, who was listening to the headset, walked over closer to the LT and said, "Six says we are to stand fast and set a perimeter. The company will link on us."

Over the next thirty minutes the LT positioned the platoon and checked the fields of fire with Sgt. Hodges. 2nd Platoon soon joined up with our left flank and 3rd joined our right. We all dug in and readied ourselves for another long night.

Chapter 12

CREATURES OF HABIT

Narrative: *Lt. McDonald-Low*

March 1968

As a platoon leader I was always on a time schedule, as were each of the platoons. Cpt. Chuck Sonata, although he was still new, was generally pretty savvy when it came to our operational plans. Sonata was 5'11" and weighed about 150 pounds dripping wet. Gaunt and pale, with a somewhat long face, he didn't look good, but no one could fault him for being dumb. He also liked to run things on a timetable.

It wasn't long before we had all settled into a routine when we were in the bush.

My day typically began at 0500 – 0530 hours, depending on the light. It was just before dawn. I was usually awakened by the final radio Sitreps (situation reports) of the night coming into our Platoon HQ from our Listening Post (LP), Observation Post (OP), and our ambush patrol. It was frequently Mac on the radio listening to each one checking in, and reporting their status. He had to listen carefully, because the small hand held AN-PRC 6 walkie-talkies that the Posts used had limited range, and voice transmissions were frequently garbled.

"Roger that Two Five Alpha. LP 2, quiet." Mac set the headset down and looked at me, "That's the last of them LT, all quiet on the Western Front. I'll get the coffee going."

"Roger that, Mac. Thanks."

Sgt. Hodges walked up to my position with his M16 slung over his shoulder, a cigarette in his mouth, holding a canteen cup filled with coffee.

"Top of the day, Lieutenant. I've got the squads pulling their Claymores and taking down the trip flares. I'll get on the horn and have the ambush patrol come on in."

"Good to go on that Sergeant. Let's get'em chowing down and ready to roll. I'll head over to Six in a few and check the plan for the day."

I knew before I reached Sonata how the day was going to shape up. It wasn't complicated in the Duc Pho AO. After a quick discussion of the day's objectives and route of travel, it was to be another day of meandering through the countryside looking for trouble. My platoon operated independently, but in concert with the others. Typically, we'd move from one small village to another and conduct searches for weapons and food caches. In the heat and humidity, with a jungle that was alive with vines, ferns, bugs, and other creatures that could bring you pain, one-quarter mile per hour was our fastest pace. The possibility of a Viet Cong sniper being around the next bend in the trail made us even more cautious.

My 2nd Squad was in the lead today and I was traveling with Sgt. Johnson's 1st Squad. Van Artsdalen was just in front of Clay, Lockhart, Zapata, Gates, and me. Sgt. Johnson, Porter, Mac, and Cerutti followed me. Porter was the "elected" officer so he had Macintyre close to him with the radio.

We were approaching a small village that was about 200 meters ahead. Most Vietnamese villagers we ran into in this AO were used to seeing heavily armed GIs. I am sure we were like the twelve-hour flu to them. We'd come in, disrupt their lives, turn their house and gardens inside out, and if they were lucky, we'd leave with nobody taken into custody, shot at, or killed. This could be tricky for them because I knew their natural instinct was to run when they saw us coming. Just one problem with that scenario, we had standing orders (and they knew) if you ran, we're going to shoot you. A rare one would run, most didn't.

Although the adult villagers could not speak English, they all did know one expression, "No VC!" It was an exclamation I heard as soon as I got to the ville'. To me it was meant to convey two different meanings. One was that they personally were not a VC and the other was there were no VC in the village. We knew it wasn't true; all villages in this area had VC guerilla forces that depended on the people for food, information, and shelter.

Sgt. Hodges had come up next to me as 1st and 3rd Squads started the search of the hooches and vicinity. Hodges rarely looked pleased, so I wasn't surprised to see him shaking his head as he looked around at the village.

"Sergeant Hodges, is there something I should know? What's going on?"

"Lieutenant, I am just highly amused by these villages we are working. In my opinion this is no place for American infantry. Our mission here could be handled by the ARVN and they would be perfect for it."

Hodges, who never had anything good to say about our South Vietnamese Army allies, surprised me with his comment. "That's pretty damn interesting hearing that from you Sergeant Hodges. If I remember correctly, the last time you referred to those soldiers you called them inoperable and spineless."

"Exactly, Lieutenant. It doesn't take much talent to be operating in this AO and let's face it, our language skills are nil and our searches are generally pointless. We make good targets for their snipers and damn little else. This a great place for the ARVN. The only thing that's good about this mission is the kids."

The children in most villages treated us much differently than the adults. They had a natural curiosity about us and they were always looking for handouts or a smile. They seemed fearless of our invasions into their lives and watched everything we did with great interest. For the most part, they were happy and seemed somewhat delighted with the strange foreign soldiers who invaded their home.

Sgt. Hodges was right about our searches. They were thorough, but crude. There would be a lot of pointing, shouting, and sign language employed to get the women and crying babies from their hooches so we could search. These one-room huts had a fire pit, cooking area, and a place for sleeping. Frequently there would also be a dirt bunker that had been dug with access to it under a wood frame bed or small table. The bunkers weren't necessarily suspicious; it just depended on the area. The more hostile the vicinity, the more bunkers we found. The Vietnamese had been at war a long time and had learned to protect themselves.

I moved with Sgt. Hodges as we watched the men conduct their searches.

"One Six, over here!" was shouted at me from the door of a hooch behind us.

It was Gates. He was standing in front of a small, grass and mud hooch, its thatch door open. I could see movement inside.

"What's the situation, Sergeant Gates?"

"We have us another bunker LT. This one is big. I can hear kids and women crying down there. We were waiting for you to proceed."

"Good job, Sergeant," I said, and turned to Sgt. Hodges.

"Find me a village elder so we can sign language him to go down and bring the people out of the bunker. I don't want someone getting killed for no reason."

Hodges immediately left on his search and it wasn't forty-five seconds later he returned with a frail looking man in tow. I had no idea how old he was, but his face was wrinkled and cracked like old leather, and he was chewing betel nut with his gums. His hair was white and he had a small, thin gray mustache.

"Here ya go, LT. One village elder."

"Good job, Top. Please employ your sign language skills and convince this old bastard to go down and get the people to come up."

Hodges, a man of few wasted words was well up to the task. After some chest tapping, pointing, and "No, no" and "Yes, yes," Hodges convinced the little old man to go down into the bunker and bring the five women and four children to the surface.

Our search of the interior of the bunker found nothing.

Villages all over Vietnam, once away from the vicinity and influence of the cities, were very primitive. No running water, no electricity, and no plumbing. For food they grew it, traded for it, found it wild, or fished for it. There were no other choices. It was no surprise we always found villages and smaller hamlets near water, no matter what AO we were working. It was the one commodity necessary for everyone. This ville' was no different.

After we had checked all the hooches, we moved out heading to our next dot on the map. Forty to sixty minutes later after being slowed by thick jungle growth, I called a halt and set a hasty perimeter. After crossing a paddy to get to the last village and then patrolling out for almost an hour, it was also sock-changing time. The infantry moves on its feet, and your feet have to stay dry to stay healthy and prevent jungle rot. Jungle rot was ulcers and other skin infections that would develop on our feet and ankles from the constant dampness. The medics were constantly busy with these types of foot problems and it was a never-ending battle.

"Delta One Six this is Six, over," I heard Sonata squawking over the radio. Macintyre leaned over and passed me the handset.

"Roger, Six, this is One Six, go."

"One Six, it's almost 1100 hours. I have just halted with Two Six elements and we're breaking for chow. Do the same. We'll resume at 1215 hours."

"Roger Six, will comply."

I smiled and passed the headset back to Mac and relayed the word to Sgt. Hodges, "Six wants us on chow break. His timing couldn't be better. We've got our usual seventy to eighty minutes to get ready to move out for the afternoon. Six will want me on the radio again in thirty minutes for the afternoon brief on direction of travel. When I've got it, you'll be the first to know. Just another afternoon in the bush, Top."

Hodges nodded his head and walked up the line heading for the squad leaders.

Just then AK fire poured into our position from three different locations. Everyone hit the ground and buried their heads as rounds impacted our perimeter.

Mac passed me the headset as elements of the platoon began to return fire. Our M-16 and M60 fire alternated between the hollow thunks of our M79 grenadiers lobbing grenades toward the suspected positions.

"Six, One Six. We've got fire coming from all along our front."

"Roger that, One Six. Hang tight and I'll see if I can get you some help."

AK rounds continued to pump into our position although it had slowed from our persistent return fire.

"One Six, Six. I've got some Sharks en route to us. ETA in zero five. Be prepared to pop smoke. Shark Two Niner will contact you directly."

I then heard the gunship pilot on the radio. "Delta One Six, this is Shark Two Niner."

"One Six, go."

"Roger that, One Six. I've Shark Two Five with me and we'll be on station in about zero four. Be prepared to pop smoke and give us a heading on the bad guys."

"Roger that. Standing by."

I yelled to Sgt. Gates who was in front of me with his squad. "Gates, pop smoke on my command. We've got Shark gunships on the way. Pass the word to keep everyone's head down."

Gates was soon shouting to his left and right, and off in the distance, I heard Hodges passing the word along.

"Delta One Six, Shark Two Niner. Pop smoke and ID the bad guys."

I then heard the thwop-thwop of the helicopters approaching our position.

"Roger, Two Niner. Popping smoke now. Identify color, over."

I yelled at Gates to pop smoke and within ten seconds green smoke was rising above our position.

"Delta One Six, I've got green smoke,"

"Roger Shark Two Niner, green smoke. Bad guys are seventy-five meters in front of us, west of the smoke, spread out left to right. Over."

"Got it, One Six. We are bringing the heat."

Mini-gun fire then ripped into the bush to our front, followed by 2.75" rockets slamming into the terrain. The jungle ahead of our position was literally dancing from the impacts. For the next five minutes the Shark gunships continued to work over the suspected enemy positions. It was both awesome and fierce. When I looked up, I could see the gunships with their big shark teeth spewing deadly mini-gun fire at rates up to 6,000 rounds per minute. It was loud and terrifying. I was glad to be on the right side of it. If the bad guys were there, they were in trouble. The pilot's accuracy in using our smoke IDs was remarkable, and I loved those guys for their courage and deadly aim.

Then there was silence.

"One Six, that's it for us. Hope it helped."

"Roger that, Shark Two Niner. Appreciate it."

"No problem, One Six. Our pleasure. We're off station now, good luck. This is Shark Two Niner, out."

UNACCOUNTED

As the helicopters flared off and left, it remained still. Apparently, the gunships had driven the shooters away, but I needed to check, just not immediately.

At 1215 hours we began our patrolling operations again and discovered several blood trails 100 meters to our front, but no bodies. We hurt them, but we had no idea how bad. We kept at it until approximately 1700 hours, discovering nothing more of importance. As we finished off the day patrols I started looking for and selecting our NDP (night defensive position) as we joined up with the rest of the company.

Our NDPs were always somewhat circular in formation with cover and terrain providing concealment and protection. We didn't want the company to be near any villages or hamlets, or in any exposed open area. We waited until dusk to move into our night perimeter and begin preparation of the position. Each platoon dug in and began their nightly routine.

One of my first jobs at each NDP was giving my coordinates to Delta Six so we could register artillery on our company position. We always wanted a circle of artillery fire, or fire aimed at a possible feature or trail that would aid the enemy in attacking our location, and we were cautious to do it right.

As the artillery rounds pounded around our position, the men dug their three-man fighting pits, and began eating and prepping their gear for the night. Cooking Cs was always a chore, but it was made easier by our use of C4 plastic explosive. You could cook with it, warm with it, explode things with it, and defend yourself with it. And there was plenty of it. I loved the stuff, but we always had to watch FNGs with their C4. If we had been out for a while or if it had been raining constantly, stocks of the handy explosive would run low and some dumb ass would resort to popping the back off his Claymore mine to retrieve more. This was not a great idea. The last thing we wanted to hear was a pop and fizzle from a Claymore as it failed to fire. I preferred cold coffee and hot lead if I were given a choice.

At full dusk, around 1900 hours, I briefed and sent out our night ambush patrol. Typically I sent out one squad per night for ambush patrol and usually about once every four days it would be the entire platoon. In certain areas, I also deployed an OP and LP, which were the least favorite of all nighttime jobs in the infantry.

After the patrols left the perimeter, all fighting pits then placed their Claymore mines and trip flares to the front of their pits. Sgt. Hodges and I then went to each position and verified that each pit had overlapping fields of fire with the positions to their left and right.

As we walked around the perimeter, we stopped and checked the position of Zapata who had a FNG in his position along with Milner.

"LT, we got this guy here who is our FNG superman. We say dig, he digs. We say eat, he eats. We say your turn for watch, he watches. It's a goddamn miracle. He don't say shit; he just does it. I love this Fuckin' New Guy. Look at our fightin' pit, LT. It's four mother fuckin' feet deep." Zapata was jubilant about the new man.

Sgt. Hodges had heard enough and, before I could say anything, he told Zapata, "That's real good Specialist Zapata. I am pleased that you're pleased. Now, if it wouldn't inconvenience you men, please ready yourselves for LP tonight. You three are obviously a lot more prepared than most in your squad."

As we walked away, we could hear Milner ranting in a whisper at Zapata, "You fuckin' idiot. Look what you did. You just had to say something in front of Sergeant Hodges with the LT standing there. Now, we got fuckin' LP, man. That is just beautiful."

Nobody wanted to be on an Observation or Listening Post. These small two or three man positions were isolated and on their own for the night. Armed with just their personal weapons and a radio, their job was to report enemy movement. They weren't located far away, usually about 300 to 900 feet; I liked positioning the LPs further out than the OPs with the tactic being that the LP could fall back to the OP if they heard something, and in turn all could fall back to the perimeter if in duress. They were our early warning system, and for the men working on them it was a night of nervousness and apprehension. No one slept on LP or OP.

As nautical twilight ended and full night began, the chatter from the men ended, the cigs went out, and we would begin another long routine of listening, waiting, and dozing. Each three-man pit had two men awake and one man sleeping. The sleeping was done in two-hour shifts and it had a lot to do with being as comfortable as you possibly could. One of our most favored comforts in the field was our poncho liner. It was our "sleeping bag/blanket/rain cover/mosquito shield/best friend." The poncho liner provided just enough warmth for cool tropical nights on the sides of mountains, and was still light and compact enough to easily stuff and carry. It also kept us warm in the rain and dried quickly, retaining little water. Unlike our rubber coated ponchos, which were too noisy and shiny in the rain, the poncho liner consisted of two layers of lightweight, quilted nylon encasing a polyester filling. It was soft and comfortable, olive drab on one side and camouflage on the other. It was as indispensable as C4, C-Rations, water, and luck.

UNACCOUNTED

The radios were monitored all night in the platoon and company HQs, as there were hourly situation reports from LPs, OPs, and ambush patrols. Company and battalion radio nets also reported the action 24/7. The radios soon became part of our nightly rhythm and pulse. It didn't take us long to learn that Vietnam was rarely quiet, especially in the dead of the night.

Night was different.

You hunkered at night and waited. And listened. Eyes and ears wide open, absorbed in your hyper-vigilance. Raindrops, animal calls, and plants rustling from the wind were magnified in the darkness. Any alien sound would set your nerves on edge and make the hair on the back of your arms and neck stand-up. When the moon was full, the jungle was filled with shadows, your imagination in overdrive. When there was no moon, you couldn't see your hand in front of your face. That's when you become aware of the deep, concussive rumble of thunder in the distant mountains, only it isn't thunder at all. It's the boom and echo of 1,000 pound bombs, dropped from B52s, impacting and ravaging another portion of the Ho Chi Minh Trail, and those desperate souls traveling it. But your thoughts and attention to even those sounds dull with the passage of time, and they soon become nothing more significant than the background noise of another night in the fucking shit.

If you were on ambush patrol, it wasn't just another night.

I generally liked ambush locations about 500-600 meters away from the company perimeter, usually along a trail, or an area we identified as possibly being used by the enemy for travel. Nearly all ambush sites we set were "L" shaped and squad sized. Each two or three man position was carefully selected just just before dark. The men dug shallow fighting holes to try to take advantage of any natural terrain feature. Each fighting position had fields of fire that were closely defined to the left and right so you wouldn't shoot your buddy during the ambush. Claymore mines were set facing outward on the long side of the "L," while an M60 machine gun was placed at the top of the "L," shooting up or down trail. Ambushes were rarely effective and they were always filled with high anxiety; everyone knew they were on their own for the night.

We all suffered from the long hours, lack of sleep, and the stress of staying alive.

At 0500 hours my day started all over again.

Chapter 13

AMBUSH AT THE "Y"

Narrative: *M. McDonald-Low*

2010

I fell and it startled me awake.

The scene had changed, and the image woke me as though someone had slapped me on the face. I sat on the side of the mattress, my hands clutching my knees. My throat was dry. I had seen myself running down from the "Y" trailhead with Macintyre.

I had to jump over and around GIs who had thrown themselves to the ground seeking what little cover there was. I needed to get back to the rest of my platoon and get them moving forward and firing. There is no waiting in an ambush, you have to overcome it as fast as you can. If you wait, you die.

As I ran down trail I came to Jerry Nelson, my platoon medic, who was sitting up in the middle of the trail. I saw that he had a long spring from an M16 magazine sticking out of either side of his chest. The spring was bobbing oddly up and down and Nelson was looking at it, not quite comprehending what his mind was telling him. Neither was I.

Nelson then looked at me and with a sorrowful expression and tears in his eyes said, "I'm sorry, LT. I'm really sorry."

I didn't quite understand what he was saying to me, and when I did, I grasped the compassion the man had for the men. He was apologizing for not being able to help. His terrible injuries only concerned him because it made him unable to aid the men.

"Nelson, stay down. I'm getting help."

I turned and with Mac close behind resumed my run down the trail passing Cerutti who was up and firing bursts of his M60 uphill. I saw his two ammo bearers on the ground; one obviously dead and the other wounded with his face buried in the crook of his arm. They were both covered from the expended shell casings of the M60 that were falling on them. Two other men were down trail about fifteen feet from him, both face down and dead. Both had gaping wounds out of their back.

I then heard the rattle and mechanical bang of a machine gun going off. Macintyre dove for the ground next to me. As soon as the machine gun stopped, I stood up and ran. I hadn't gone four steps when out of the corner of my eye I saw a flash.

As the rocket-propelled grenade exploded mid-trail, I was knocked off my feet and blown backwards. Small pieces of shrapnel hit me in my forearm and upper body. Another piece of shrapnel grazed my lips as I fell backwards tripping over the rock wall that guarded the dry streambed. I landed on my ass. My ears were ringing. I felt lost in the moment and everything seemed to be in slow motion.

Dazed, I picked up my M16 and looked down at the blood beginning to darken the sleeve of my jungle shirt. As I examined the stain and wondered what had happened, I noticed movement from a small, heavily camouflaged trap door as it flipped open ten feet across the trail from me. A floppy green hat attached to a dark haired, dark skinned Vietnamese followed it. He looked right at me. I looked back at him so hard it felt like my eyes were going to pop out of my head; I could hear the blood pumping in my ears.

As he stood up waist high in his "spider hole," I saw his .22 carbine come up next, point and blast away at me on full auto. Two rounds hit my M16 and blew it out of my hands, while sending small fragments into my right forearm and chest. Two other rounds hit me in the right shoulder and bicep knocking me onto my back. Other rounds blew just past my head.

My nightmare continued.

Chapter 14

AN AMERICAN WITNESS

M. McDonald-Low

2010

EMAIL

Michael McDonald-Low to Ray Carne, JPAC

30 Aug 2010

Mr. Carne,

Is there an update on the Van Artsdalen search? I did not hear back from you after supplying coordinates and info.

Please advise,

Michael McDonald-Low

———

EMAIL

Carne, Ray Civ JPAC J2 to Michael McDonald-Low

2 Sept 2010

Michael,

How's your schedule looking for next June? It looks like we need some eyewitness help. The team went again to the location on

Nui Hoac Ridge previously supplied by C. Sonata. This is obviously incorrect.

You're now officially an American Witness for JPAC and you will head the search for 1165. Welcome to the team! Please keep me informed of any medical condition, situation, or medications that we need to be aware of. The team will consist of 12 members to include a Special Forces medic.

Your timeline: Mid May – Mid June is mission period. TDY period: 10–15 days.

May and June are very hot…I'm sure I don't have to tell you. Once we get you in country the team will work together side by side with the Vietnamese officials.

If you need any additional maps, let me know. I'm building the lead requirement based on your information. There are certain restrictions and conditions that we must consider when putting a lead together. Basically the Vietnamese will find us a shortest route to your location; based on the cost of land clearing. That is why we have to be very precise when selecting a location to survey. I know that will be difficult because of the terrain alterations.

Please start a PT program now if you don't already have one. Your safety is our priority.

I'm very hopeful that this will be a successful mission.

Ray

———

EMAIL
Michael McDonald-Low to Carne, Ray Civ JPAC J2
3 Sept 2010

Ray,

Thanks for the info. I look forward to participating.

I am in good shape and I am confident I will receive a go-ahead from my VA doc. I work out with weights 3 days a week and walk every day. I will be ready for the heat and the hump.

I am curious about gear. What can or should I bring?

The maps – I would like the best (highest detail) topography maps we can get for that area. If we have sat pics, that would be good, too.

Just a few early thoughts.

Michael

———

EMAIL
Carne, Ray Civ JPAC J2 to Michael McDonald-Low
3 Sept 2010

Michael,

As for equipment, we will issue you a complete list of necessary items shortly.

UNACCOUNTED

Since this case Province is in Quang Nam, I will request the team to conduct an investigation in Quang Nam Province, first.

I will send the leads to the Socialist Republic of Vietnam 60 days prior to the execution of the mission. Once they tell me that they will support it that's when we get the green flag to put 1165 on the list. There is no doubt, they shouldn't say no to 1165.

On the day of the investigation for 1165 the lead analyst will take charge on how to conduct the investigation. Once you arrive at the Vehicle Dismount Point (VDP), you will be the point man for the team. Unfortunately as I stated earlier, the officials will arrange the trail. We have no control over that. Once arrive at your location, you will advise the analyst on how far and where to look once you get familiar with the terrain.

After you identify the location the team will begin their search and investigation.

There will be no official excavation at this time; the mission is to locate. Once we put out a report and brief the command in Hawaii, they will make the decision for the excavation. If a positive decision is made then a recovery team will come out and conduct a full excavation for 30 days with an anthropologist in a future mission.

After your investigation is completed, I will fly you commercially from Vietnam back to Hawaii for debrief. You will stay in Oahu for two days and then fly back home, mission accomplished.

That's pretty much what you are to expect. If you have any more questions, I am here to answer them for you.

Ray

Chapter 15

LIFE IN THE ZOO

Narrative: *Spec. 4 Clifford Van Artsdalen*

8 - 10 April 1968

On 8 April 1968, at 0540 hours, Delta Company and the other companies of the 11th Light Infantry Brigade began Operation Norfolk Victory, an offensive sweep in the mountainous, heavily forested terrain west of Nghia Hanh, Quang Ngai. Launching from a staging area on LZ Dragon, the operation was initiated by the combat air assaults of five rifle companies. It was our biggest operation to date, and our first prolonged foray into the mountains southeast of the Que Son Valley.

Over the first two days of Operation Norfolk Victory we maneuvered through the rugged, brushy terrain of the foothills. On the afternoon of the second day, we found a large hooch that contained thousands of pounds of rice, dozens of NVA ponchos, chickens, fish sauce, and rolls of waterproof material. It was apparent to all of us that the NVA were thick in the area and we were just getting started in the hills that led to the dark, green peaks of 900 and 1400-meter tall mountains. We were heading there.

That night the company was laagered on the slope of a small hill that was heavily canopied and rich with jungle vegetation. We had found a small clearing and had set a perimeter along the edge. We had no enemy contact through the course of the day, and given the seclusion of our location, we expected little trouble that night. I remember the jungle being alive with sounds that evening when at 2230 hours all hell broke loose on our upward slope perimeter positions near 2nd Platoon. I heard screeching, and then yelling, and suddenly Claymore's were going off and M16 fire had opened up from the 2nd. As I leaned over the edge of my fighting pit, Clay and Lockhart next to me, I heard more screeching and commotion. I then heard, "It's fuckin' monkeys!"

Dozens of monkeys had torn through 2nd Platoon's position and had then ripped through the entire company. One ran past our position not three feet away; a dark blur in the night, screaming at us as it ran by. After the initial excitement of the monkey invasion, I listened to the GIs laughing around me.

Big Todd was particularly amused, "Boy, I ain't ever seen a monkey, 'cept on TV. Those fuckers are quick. I'm surely glad those bastards ain't armed. We all be in a world of shit, boy."

"You got that right, big man. They're quick, and those monkeys don't know nothin' 'bout being afraid. They just tore ass through here," Clay said laughing. Cerutti in the next pit over was doubled-up in laughter.

Not twenty feet away in the Platoon HQ pit, Macintyre had been listening to the commentary and I heard him say to Sgt. Hodges, Nelson and the LT, "The men are amused by the monkeys, but I've got a better story. I heard it from a sergeant from the 1st Air Cav I met when we were at Charley Brown. He was with E Battery, Aviation, 82nd Arty."

By then Macintyre had my complete attention, as well as all nearby fighting pits. I waited for him to continue with his tale. I knew it would be good. Mac always had a smart-ass college boy perspective. I leaned forward out of my pit so I could hear him better.

"Apparently the Cav was on stand-down at Camp Evans. Well, one night they get rocketed and in the morning when they check the perimeter, this Cav grunt finds a wounded brown monkey. The guy scoops him up in his ruck and carries him back to camp where he nurses it back to health with the help of his platoon medic. He names the monkey Cocoa. Every day the guy feeds Cocoa and gives him water. Check this, the monkey apparently is so grateful to this grunt for saving him they become great friends. The monkey follows him everywhere. The grunt soon taught the monkey how to smoke and drink beer. Cocoa even got his own miniature rucksack so he could help the grunt carry ammo and water. Well, the first time this grunt takes the monkey with him on patrol, as luck would have it, the patrol comes under intense machine gun and AK fire. When the grunt looks around for Cocoa, he saw that the monkey had already dropped the rucksack and fled back into the jungle."

Macintyre paused for about five seconds, and then with a deadpan expression he said, "The moral of this story is that monkeys are not as dumb as they apparently seem."

For me it was just another had to be there moment, and I was smiling and laughing under my breath when I heard Cerutti say laughing, "Makes you wanna be a fuckin' monkey and get the fuck outta here." He then turned toward Macintyre and in a loud whisper said, "That's good shit, Mac. Who said a college boy ain't funny?"

Zapata in his surly way did not appreciate the monkey humor, "Yeah, it's just fuckin' hilarious, Macintyre. This place is like being in a fuckin' zoo, man."

Roosevelt just laughed. I didn't think it was so funny.

Snakes, lizards, birds, spiders, and leeches were just part of the scenery and struggles for us in the bush, but nobody was dumb enough to be curious about big spiders or snakes of any kind, which we rarely saw. We did face other hazards though, that had no heartbeats. The worst was elephant grass.

UNACCOUNTED

Elephant grass could kill you. Elephant grass grew seven feet tall in Vietnam and covered hundreds of meters of jungle terrain. The tall, green blades of elephant grass had edges as sharp as razors. If you were in it and trying to move by cutting or crawling your way through it, the heat and humidity held in the grass would damn near suffocate you. It happened to us during our fourth day of Norfolk Victory, the day after the monkey attack. We had just combat air assaulted to location not five minutes away when we received sniper fire from a small hill on a ridge not far from where we landed. It sounded as though it was coming from two locations on the hill, but it was difficult to read. The hill looked as if it topped out at about 200 meters, and it was all elephant grass. I heard from the LT that Delta Six had ordered the platoons to engage and move to the top of the hill. Our company of three platoons started up through the grass, each trying to stay abreast as we moved up the hill. It lasted for about five minutes. We weren't fifty meters up that hill before we had men falling out from the heat as they tried to move and cut their way through the seven-foot tall grass.

It wasn't long before I had the LT right behind me.

"Jesus, Van Artsdalen. Where's the top of this thing?" the LT said, gasping for air. His face and hands were bloody from the cuts inflicted by the elephant grass. He looked drained, and Mac looked even worse. I was surprised to see them, as they were usually farther back from the lead squad.

"LT, this grass has damned near killed everyone on the way up. Clay and Big Todd were the last to go. Sergeant Gates is up front still pushing."

"Roger that. I passed Lockhart and Clay when I passed the last of 3rd Squad. Doc Nelson and Doc Kotsaris have their hands full."

When we reached the top of the hill there were a total of seven guys who had made it: the LT, Mac, Lt. Seifert from 2nd Platoon, Sgt. Martz the 2nd Platoon Sergeant, Sgt. Gates, Sgt. Hodges, and me. Everyone was soaked from head to foot with sweat and blood from the cuts we had all endured to get through the elephant grass. We were lucky no NVA had remained behind at the top to wait for our "company" attack of seven men.

One hour and twenty-five minutes later, we had finally gotten everyone off the hill and out of the smothering grass. It took the company the rest of the day and night to recover. We even had a special resupply when Delta Six demanded that we needed water to continue to do our jobs effectively.

The Big Six's all liked that; the attitude, the hunger for success, the willingness to extend yourself.

Some soldiers did not feel the same way. Cerutti was particularly pissed off as he dug in that night. It was raining heavily. "I hate this fucking shit hole. Look at where we are, absolutely in the middle of fucking nowhere. Rain pounding up our ass, mud in all my shit. My hands are cut to pieces from that fuckin' grass. I cannot remember what it's like to be dry. I just want to kill those mother fuckers and get the fuck outta here."

"Listen to you, man," Zapata said as he was bent over, digging. "You talkin' shit, pissin' and moanin'. What good does it do you? I know you're feelin' bad about the rain, the mud, the life, but shit, it don't mean nothin', homey. You know that shit happens."

Cerutti paused and closed his eyes for a moment. He was holding his entrenching shovel, his M60 was on the edge of his pit, its tripod glistening black, rain droplets shining on its spine. His jungle pants and bare chest were mud smeared, and his dog tags dripped from the sweat of his labor. He had a five-day beard, and his face was filthy and streaked with mud and sweat. His hair stood out in all directions. Suddenly he started laughing. As he opened his eyes he pointed his entrenching shovel at Zapata and with a broad smile said, "Zapata, you are absolutely right. It ain't no big thang. It is perfectly fuckin' perfect. I love this place, Zapman. I mean, I really LOVE this place."

Cerutti then looked up at the darkening sky. He paused for a few moments and shook his head slowly. He then bent over and went back to digging. He didn't say another word.

Chapter 16

Narrative: *Spec. 4 Clifford Van Artsdalen*
11 April 1968

The next morning First Platoon was again walking point for the company and it had started quietly enough. We were moving slowly up the mid-base of a giant ridge and hill. The terrain was steep and canopy covered; small trees, ferns, vines and big leafy plants were drooping from the rain.

As I quietly moved through the wet bush, I stopped, almost bumping into Sgt. Gates. He looked at me with that "what the fuck?" expression on his face. Just then we both heard an M79 buckshot round go off to our front. It was Jimmy Slatten. He was the point man and obviously had seen something. Gates and I both rushed forward passing Cerutti and his M60 crew and then Clay, Lockhart, Zapata, and Milner.

When we got to Slatten he was crouched and signaled us to get down and come forward. When we were next to him he whispered, "I peeked my head through some big elephant ears and I bumped right into the face of a fuckin' NVA. Just as he raised his AK at me I blew a hole right through him. He's right over there."

Sgt. Gates stood up and peered through the elephant ears and then squatted back down beside us.

Roosevelt, Alex, and two other guys, Lockhart and Zapata, quickly joined our position, weapons at the ready. I then heard more movement downhill from us and heard Vietnamese chatter.

"Down," Gates ordered in a whisper.

We listened. In the triple canopy jungle and forest, the ambient daytime light was dim at best and the jungle was usually alive with sounds. Now, it was quiet. I could still hear the dinks, and they sounded like they were moving away from us.

I looked over to where the buckshot round of the M79 had blown a hole though the foliage where the enemy soldier had stood. The blackened leaves formed a halo around the hole. The smell of cordite was still thick in the air. Seconds later Lt. McDonald-Low and his RTO, Macintyre came up and squatted beside Sgt. Gates. He listened to Gates' report.

Then I heard him call the CO on the handset.

"Delta Six, this is One Six, over."

"This is Six, go."

"We have killed what appears to be the lead element of an NVA force. I can hear a bunch of dinks talking and moving away from us. They're about 100 meters from our position. The dink here had a pack, rice, a can of fish sauce, and is in full uniform. Armed with an AK47, over."

"Roger One Six, good job. Proceed to advance and engage. Keep pushing, over."

The LT then got us moving, and within 500 meters we came upon an elaborate NVA camp spread out on either side of a stream. As the rest of the company hurried to join us, the LT fanned the platoon out to secure the area. We soon discovered that the camp was large enough to be a company sized bivouac and training area. It had obviously just been hastily evacuated as cooking fires were still going, and their gear was strewn throughout the area. There were banners hung in the trees and NVA flags openly displayed. Delta Six and the remainder of the company soon joined us at the camp and a full search began.

I had just moved to the far end of the camp when AK fire started blasting away at us from the jungle above. Everyone in my squad returned fire. The LT moved 3rd Squad over to join us and soon a running gun battle had erupted. All of 1st Platoon was in hot pursuit of an unknown number of NVA that had moved from their initial position, and were now running downhill about 500 meters from us. As we watched, we saw them circle back up an adjacent ridgeline and head for the upper reaches of the hill off to our right front. It was no hill. It looked like a green mountain that headed straight up and into the mist. The LT called it Hill 922, because it was 922 meters tall. It looked like an ass kicker to me.

The LT stopped our pursuit and called a hasty meeting of the squad leaders and Sgt. Hodges. I was close enough to learn that Six had commanded the LT to have 1st Platoon regain contact with the NVA and track them up Hill 922. I knew that 1st Squad would be leading as Gates had already started to move with Roosevelt, Lockhart, Zapata, Porter, and Cerutti with the rest of us close behind. Sgt. Moore, our squad leader, followed along with the rest of the squad and platoon.

We moved slowly, as the rest of the platoon was trailing us, and we didn't want to be too far ahead. After about thirty minutes, we stopped. We had just reached a point where the ridgeline had widened out and dramatically steepened. I saw a well-used trail running straight up the ridge through the dense jungle. Lt. McDonald-Low, who had just arrived next to me called the platoon to a halt behind him. Gates, Roosevelt, and Macintyre joined us. We all crouched behind a rock. Off to our left, not fifty meters away, the cliff appeared to drop off into nothingness. I crawled and peered over the edge and discovered a small, rocky outcropping that was about ten by ten feet. Beyond this small apron it dropped another 200 feet to the tops of the trees of the ridge below.

UNACCOUNTED

The LT called Delta Six, and he was told to dig in and hold our position for the night while they finish searching and clearing the base camp. The LT brought up the rest of the platoon, and he and Sgt. Hodges set the defensive perimeter with three man positions. Roosevelt, Lockhart, and I were on the extreme left flank just up from where it dropped off. Sgt. Hodges passed the word that 2nd Platoon had been ordered to find a way up the backside of 922, come over the top and link with us; hopefully trapping the NVA in the middle. 3rd Platoon would remain with Six at the base camp, continue to search, and act as a reserve reaction force.

Artillery registration by the LT and the forward observer who was with us began as soon as we started digging. Everyone always held their breath on the first round, but the LT did not miss. I watched as they laid in fire up slope from us at several points about 350 and 500 meters distant.

Looking over to where the LT and command group had picked their position I could hear the radio "squawking." It was a sound we all got used to. You would first hear a deep hiss and then a distant, hollow sounding voice calling out for Delta Six or Delta One Six, the LT.

"Crossbow Delta One Six, this is Crossbow Delta Three, over."

Delta Three was the company Executive Officer, Lt. Handley, calling for the platoon's resupply list and updating the LT on HQ bullshit.

"This is One Six, go."

"Roger One Six, pass me to One Seven when we're done. I've got some news for him on R&Rs coming up, and we have some new guys we're getting ready to send your way when we can."

"Roger that. How many am I getting and what are they?"

"This is Three. You'll be getting two 11Bs and an E-5 with experience. You've also got two men going on R & R. Lewis and McCarthy. Three Six is going, too. Could be worse, over."

"I roger that, Three. Hang loose and I'll track down my One Seven."

The LT turned and told his RTO, "Mac, find Sergeant Hodges and have him get on the horn with the XO."

"On it already, LT. I know right where he is."

As Macintyre took off in the direction of our right flank, I got serious about digging in. With us just knocking over that NVA base camp, I expected trouble. I also thought when the word got out, everyone would be seriously jealous of McCarthy and Lewis. Everyone in Vietnam was permitted one R&R (Rest and Recreation) during their one-year tour of duty and it was their turn, just at the right time. Lucky bastards.

At 1805 hours, the LT spread the word that Delta Six reported the company had found fifty-two weapons at the NVA camp that included rifles, machine guns, and a bunch of ammo. We had definitely caught them by surprise.

As it turned to dusk, and while we were chowing down, our perimeter was raked by automatic weapons' fire from uphill. As I looked to my right front, I saw two NVA soldiers running up the ridge trail, stopping, and shooting again. All along our front, guys were yelling, pointing, and shooting as more AK rounds zinged over our heads. 2nd Squad and part of 3rd Squad, positioned on the upper right side of our perimeter, erupted into fire after the fleeing NVA. I shot as well and thought I had a pretty good bead on them. It was over as quickly as it had started. The AK fire had stopped and no one on our side was hit.

The LT soon had artillery falling on the upper slope of 922, and while we listened to the big booms above we soon returned to eating and making final touches to our fighting pits for the night. It looked like we were going to need them.

Sgt. Hodges was not eating or digging in, but was instead chewing the ass out of Sgt. Johnson. "Johnson, what in the fuck were you doing when those dinks were shooting at us? The reason why I ask is that I know what you should have been doing, and we both know you weren't. I watched you. Your ass was hugging the dirt, Sergeant."

Sgt. Johnson, my squad leader, had not distinguished himself during our brief engagement. When the NVA had first fired at our position, everyone grabbed their weapons and looked to return fire as they were hitting the ground. We were all looking for targets to engage. Sgt. Johnson, our Korean War vet and "show off," had done the opposite and jumped into a completed fighting pit and covered his head. He had also left his weapon on the ground in front of the pit from where he had jumped. He never attempted to fight. I saw it. Roosevelt and Sgt. Gates saw it. The whole 1st Squad saw it. Worst of all, Lt. McDonald-Low saw it, and now he stood next to Hodges.

"Sergeant Johnson. It was your responsibility to lead your squad at all times, not just when it is convenient or quiet. Sergeant Hodges is exactly right. It is unacceptable to me and most of all, to your men."

Sgt. Johnson was relieved of his position as squad leader and would be transferred to the company HQ when convenient. In other words, he was to stay out of the way. Apparently, the LT did not believe in second chances when it came to leadership. To my surprise and delight, Sgt. Gates was given command of the squad.

UNACCOUNTED

We all hunkered down nervously for the night as it began to rain, again.

Chapter 17

LET'S KICK SOME ASS

Narrative: *Lt. McDonald-Low*

12 - 13 April 1968

On my first morning on the side of Nui Ky Lan - Hill 922, I had the platoon pull its Claymores and I sent three men from each squad fifteen meters forward of our night position for a quick look-see. I soon heard that 2nd Squad found some expended brass from an AK. Randall Milner and Jimmy Slatten of Gates' squad then yelled that they had found a blood trail. Nearby they found a pack containing rice, a money belt with documents, and a diary with twenty-two envelopes with stamps. There was no weapon found.

Back at the base camp, Captain Sonata, the HQ element and 3rd Platoon had continued to sweep the area and had found and searched twenty-five straw hooches, all of which had been recently occupied. In the encampment they found military equipment for thirty or more soldiers, Ho Chi Minh banners, two small radios (like our PRC 6s), documents, and medical supplies. Delta Six later reported they also had found an anti-tank grenade, six Chi Com grenades, and a B-40 rocket launcher, in addition to the other weapons discovered the day before.

While Delta Six continued to search the base camp with his HQ group, forward observer, and one squad of 3rd Platoon, Seifert's 2nd, and Swan's 3rd Platoon, now led by SFC Harrison, maneuvered their units all day. 3rd Platoon eventually moved into a blocking position on the west side of the ridge, while 2nd Platoon moved northward up the ridge trying to move to the top of 922. We continued to hold the southern ridge of 922 about 600 meters from the top.

That afternoon, we made our first probe of 922. I put out two flanking squads with one squad and HQ up the middle, which is where I wanted to be for control. Mac was on my ass as we started our deployment to move uphill, "LT, Six wants to know our location and progress as we move up the hill."

"Good luck with that Mac, I think you know we'll have our heads down the whole way."

I then heard Mac, as I had grown accustomed to, call Sonata, "Roger, Six. This is Delta One Six Alpha, will comply."

Mac looked at me and winked. "No problem, LT, we're good to go and it is copacetic with Six."

I nodded and looked at Sgt. Hodges, "Let's move."

Hodges, ever the diplomat, looked to his left and right and said, "All right you bad boys, let's get our fuckin' asses up that hill. Earn your money!"

It was daunting to assault uphill in such steep terrain, as it forced us to climb and crawl in small spurts over and under fallen trees, thick, leafy bushes and vines. It was also wet and muddy. We'd crawl fifteen feet forward and then slide back ten in the mud. It also took a lot of energy in the extreme heat and humidity to maintain the drive to not just move forward, but up and forward. And of course, you're doing it with an M16 in your hand, a lifeline of a different kind. This is when your mind examines things that you normally wouldn't. As time slows down, you find your face in the mud as you listen to the AK fire skimming the air above your head. It's coming from those mother fuckers in their entrenched positions that you cannot, for the life of you, see. You push uphill; mud oozing between your fingers, blood on your knuckles. There's a shout from someone across from you, but all you can do is smell the ozone, cordite, and the green, goddamn jungle.

My M16 was a disaster as I wiped mud from the flash suppressor. "Not real good," I thought, as I pulled the weapon back to me and used a stick to unplug the clogged trigger housing and muzzle.

I then looked across at Van Artsdalen and saw him gesture at me as he yelled, "LT, my '79' rounds are goin' no where in this fuckin' jungle. They just get slapped down and I've almost stepped on two of the duds."

Sgt. Hodges, after crawling and sliding back from the left flank, was now next to me looking at Mac hugging the mud, being small. "We've got some real issues. The M60s are getting major heat cause the '79' gunners can't suppress the dink fire. We were making pretty good progress, but now we're not making any headway. They've redirected their fire and have us pinned down here, and it looks like 2nd Squad on the right is having a tough go. The good news is that 3rd Squad overran two small positions on the left flank, and think they killed four or five before withdrawing."

The dense vegetation had made one of our most important weapons ineffective. The M79s didn't work because the brush, vines, ferns, and trees would knock the grenades down before they would have a chance to arm themselves. The 79's buckshot rounds were ineffective at any range beyond five meters, and in this terrain they were virtually worthless. The guys carrying them felt unarmed, usually because the only other weapon they carried was a .45 caliber pistol, which was great at fifteen feet, but not so good beyond that distance.

My original plan was to move three squads in fire and movement, attacking in a three-pronged assault. I wanted the squads in a three-man front to cover more terrain and to get more firepower up front, but the ridge was so steep and foggy with mist that we couldn't see each other, or our advance. Consequently, the platoon ended up in an upside down "U" shape and we had lost our ability to front enough men to gain an advantage in firepower. The squads on the far ends of the "U" were staggered 50 meters down the sharp, knife-edged ridgeline of 922 on both sides, barely able to move because of the steepness, mud, and the sheer impossibility of the jungle. The middle of the assault group and the M60s were catching so much NVA fire that they could only advance in small, slow spurts and now were stopped.

Our first assault of 922 sputtered and then came to a halt. I could tell our momentum had stopped because of where our fire was coming from, as infrequent as it had become. I also heard the call for "Medic!" from somewhere near the flank of the platoon, downhill, and left of my position with 1st Squad.

Sgt. Hodges then yelled at me, "Incoming grenades!"

I looked up and saw two ChiCom grenades floating in the air, uphill from our position. Luckily, the grenades didn't do much as they were slapped down by the vegetation and exploded twenty-five feet above our position.

I looked up from the mud and then shouted at Sgt. Hodges, "I think we've got issues up in the front now and over near 2nd Squad. Yell at Gates and tell him to pull 1st Squad slowly back downhill and meet up with us next to 2nd."

Hodges nodded at me and scrambled off down over the hill to my right and then up toward where Gates was. I soon heard him shouting at Gates to pull back. Just then a hail of AK fire exploded near where Hodges was headed. I then saw Hodges scramble and low crawl back to us, moving like a snake through the mud and slime.

As he tumbled in and over a small mound in front of where Mac and I were hunkering down, he landed on his ass. Undeterred as usual, Hodges said in a calm voice, "Got the word to Gates, LT. They're gonna be a minute. Slatten has been killed and they're having to drag him. Porter has been hit too, but he's moving. Let's get the hell outta here."

Going downhill and across the ridge was much easier than going up. It was easy to slide through the mud and low scrub, ferns, and small banana-leafed vegetation. It was chaos when we made it to our original starting point. The NVA small arms' fire had been vicious in the front, and the push up the flanks had caught a lot of heat as well. Members of 2nd and 3rd Squad also had casualties. One of the men was headshot and two others had suffered multiple frag wounds from a grenade.

Nelson was busy assessing each man as he came to them and was applying appropriate field dressings by priority. He had plenty of help as men of both squads assisted him.

The automatic weapons' fire began again uphill from us where Gates' men were positioned. I then saw Van Artsdalen and Porter come slithering over a small ridge and out of the bushes towards us. Lockhart and Zapata soon followed them dragging the lifeless Slatten. The entire back of Slatten's head was missing. I saw that Porter had a bloody field bandage wrapped around his arm. He looked wobbly. Clay and two other men soon appeared from above, but stopped and turned around taking up defensive positions.

"Lockhart, Clay, and I had three dinks come up on us from the far flank where 2nd Squad had been," Gates yelled at me. "I think we killed all three, but we could see movement up above. I've left Cerutti with three others up there to cover our asses, LT."

Suddenly, the NVA fire just stopped. It was easy to tell, because there weren't any more rounds whizzing over our heads. Gradually, the M60 fire from Cerutti and the others slowed and then died.

Sgt. Hodges looked at me from his position behind a tree by Clay, "Lieutenant, the fight has gone out of those dinks.

We need to get our wounded out and develop a better course of action."

I then pulled all three squads back with the casualties. We moved downhill to our previous night defensive position where we had left our rucksacks and gear. I left two men from each squad to cover our movement, and they would remain there until dusk.

I was able to get a helicopter in to our location when it finally stopped raining late that afternoon. We needed both ammo and water, and we had two dead and three wounded to get out. The small, rocky apron next to our position was just wide enough to allow the chopper to settle on one skid and hover. To my surprise, it was none other than Budweiser Six who was commanding the bird. He waved at me as we loaded the casualties on board. I gave him a salute and wondered why he had personally come instead of another working slick. I learned a few days later that he was nominated for a Silver Star for his "bravery" in making that run to me, which was done in the clear; we were receiving no enemy fire. I put two and two together and just figured that the Big Six needed some medals to go with the body count we were beginning to rack up. Ain't no big thang.

That night the FO and I hit the hill again with 105 artillery fire. I was hoping to soften up the NVA, but more importantly keep them from coming down on us in the dark.

It apparently worked, though I doubt any of the troops caught any extra sleep.

The next day we again probed the upper reaches of 922 looking for weaknesses and ways to overcome the NVA positions. Each time we would crawl through the mud, foot by foot uphill, only to end up sliding and rolling downhill under fire from the NVA. It was messy, frustrating and dangerous, but we were also starting to get a feel for our attack routes, and more importantly where the best cover was located. We suffered casualties each time.

Mac kept me updated on the progress of 2nd Platoon and told me Seifert on the other side of 922 was having a tough go in even steeper terrain. He also learned that while the platoon was trying to gain a foothold on the steep rocky hillside, Lt. Seifert took some shrapnel from a ChiCom grenade and fell about fifteen feet. Wounded with an injured leg and wrist, he had made it back to Six's location for Dust Off, and Sgt. Martz was now running the platoon.

I was glad for John. I was thinking about how he had that "million dollar" wound he was always joking about when the issue of how to get to the top of 922 became clear to me. We needed more firepower. A lot more. We needed something that would knock down the vegetation and penetrate uphill to their fighting positions. Something that would suppress their weapons and grenade fire, and have them keep their heads down as we moved uphill.

I knew what that something was.

Chapter 18

PLANTING THEM IN ROWS

Narrative: *Spec. 4 Clifford Van Artsdalen*

14 April 1968

Finally on 14 April, at approximately 0900 hours, in a thick mist, we assaulted 922 again with the use of a 90mm M67 Recoilless Rifle that the LT had brought in earlier that morning.

The slick that brought the rifle and its three-man crew had landed on the same precarious apron we had used many times earlier. When I watched the three offload the "90" and three big wooden crates of ammo, I wondered what was going on. I had never seen the stovepipe styled black tube other than in demonstrations at AIT, and its ammo crates were almost three feet long.

The LT quickly directed the three men off the apron with their gear and moved them up near our squad's dug-in positions. They all had clean uniforms and their boots were shined. They were obviously from a rear base unit, probably a specialized combat engineer team. They also looked nervous as hell. I doubted that any of them had ever imagined being out where we were.

As I watched them unpack the ammo boxes, I saw that each contained four huge buckshot shells. I doubt they were called that, but I knew what a buckshot shell looked like, though I had never seen one nineteen inches long and weighing four pounds. They were gigantic. The rifle itself was almost five feet long and it looked weighty the way they were lugging it around.

I listened as the LT briefed the three. I wanted to hear what he had in mind for the strange weapon. I know we needed help. My squad had already lost four men, all of them my friends.

"It's good to see you men. I'm Lieutenant McDonald-Low and this is Sergeant Hodges," he said, referring to Hodges who had just joined them.

The shorter of the three stepped forward and with a deep southern drawl said, "Nice to meet y'all, Lieutenant. This here's Specialist's Stacy and Warren. I'm Sergeant Galvin, your gunner. We've brought twelve Canister rounds as instructed, but I have to tell you Lieutenant, we ain't never been out here with infantry in the bush. Watcha y'all have in mind for us?"

"Sergeant Galvin, we're going to assault straight uphill using your 90 to punch holes through the jungle. Its firepower will give us the momentum we need. It's been tough for us to get a foothold when we're constantly having to keep our heads down."

"Well, Lieutenant you've got the right men for the job. We will gladly put some fire on their butts. Just keep us covered, we ain't used to being put upon," Galvin said with a look of concern.

Sgt. Hodges looked at Galvin and his two ammo bearers and as expected replied, "Don't you men worry about shit that could possibly happen. We will keep their fuckin' heads down so you will have the luxury of laying waste to their positions. The LT and I will be right next to you directing your fire. Relax, son. We've been here a while."

With those words, Galvin nodded and quickly went about readying the weapon as the ammo bearers loaded big canvas slings with the canister rounds.

After positioning the 90 in the middle of 1st and 2nd Squads, the LT began our assault on 922 with the first volley from the 90. We quickly saw that the huge gaps created by the 90's buckshot rounds not only cleared brush, they also chewed up the mud. It was weird, too. At the thunderous sound of the first round going off, and the flames shooting fifteen feet out the back of the 90 with a giant "whoosh," the NVA fire immediately began to slacken from their entrenched positions above. I guess the NVA had never seen or heard anything like the 90 and its flaming thunder. It was not surprising, as it was shooting the same size ammunition that our tanks used. I'm sure it scared the hell out of them.

For the next two hours we gradually blasted our way uphill, punching holes through foliage and brush until we reached the last of their abandoned fighting positions. It had been slow going, and no one was in a hurry, especially the LT. He and Sgt. Hodges kept the platoon tight and online, crawling and rushing forward with each blast of the 90. It was shoot, move fifty meters, stop, and shoot the 90 again. We used all twelve rounds from that big gun to help us reach the last of their positions.

As we searched the now deserted NVA positions, I heard that 3rd Platoon, after joining and relieving the 2nd, had begun an assault from the opposite side of 922 when we did. They encountered light resistance, reporting that the dinks had withdrawn soon after hearing the booms of the 90 coming up the other side. It was over.

When the fog and mist had finally cleared that morning, our platoon was instructed by the battalion commander to do a body count and search for weapons. We were to dig up all graves should we find any. We found many. In total, we dug up twenty-seven hasty gravesites and verified our body count; fifteen had been killed by artillery and the rest by small arms' fire. None of them had weapons or any personal effects.

It was grisly work for a holiday. In truth, it was such an ugly business that when we reburied the enemy dead, we did it so the NVA would notice we had been there and were responsible. The LT had us remove and position their "Ho Chi Minh" sandals, which is what we called their military flip-flops, so they stuck out of the ground. They were all neatly planted in rows. Later that morning, at 1130 hours, 3rd Platoon walked down from 922 to join us at our position. You could hear the laughter when their lead elements encountered the sandals marking the NVA dead.

It's strange what happens in war that makes you laugh.

Later that morning, after returning to our NDP, I listened to the LT as he talked with our sister company, Charlie Company, who I was surprised to learn were also located on 922, but on the part of the ridgeline that ran down to our east.

"Charlie Six, Delta One Six, over."

"Charlie Six, here. How the hell are you, Mike?"

"Real good, Six. We're just finishing off over here as I'm sure you know. I'm surprised to hear you're so close. We've been busy."

"Roger that, One Six. We joined the party yesterday and we've been working on this underground hospital and base camp we found over here on the east side. Apparently, this whole area is one big NVA facility for rest, rearming and planning."

"I hear you on that, Six. We walked right in on them on this side. We were the last thing they expected."

"One Six, we're knee-deep in the hospital right now, and I need to run. You guys take care, and we'll see you in the air or on the ground. I heard there's something big beginning to build up over near LZ Center. The 196th took some real punishment there so watch your ass. Six out."

I wondered what that something "big" was and what would happen next. I also had a feeling I wouldn't have to wait long for the answer.

During the seven days of the operation, Delta's body count of NVA was reported at fifty-six. I thought that figure was a little high, because our platoon did most of the fighting. We had kicked their ass, but at a real cost. Delta Company suffered three KIA and twelve WIA. Most of the casualties were in 1st Platoon and in 1st Squad, Jimmy Slatten and Bob Banks were both killed, Porter was fragged from a grenade, and T. Smith was shot in the arm and shoulder. All of them were my buddies and part of our original crew from Hawaii.

Chapter 19

BAD WATER AND BLOOD TIES

Narrative: *Lt. McDonald-Low*

15 April – 4 May 1968

The next morning, we pulled off 922 and joined Cpt. Sonata, the company headquarters elements, and 2nd Platoon at the NVA base camp. Jerry Swan, the 3rd Platoon leader had left on R&R, and John Seifert, 2nd's Platoon leader had been dusted off after falling in 2nd's trying climb to the top of 922. Chuck was using the 2nd as his private "go-fer" platoon and the 3rd Platoon he had placed under Sergeant Martz.

Sonata looked tired. Chuck was not the healthiest looking of guys to begin with, and he looked particularly drained now.

"One Six, good to see you guys, We just found another hidden hooch filled with radios and rice. This place was loaded with their supplies, but I think that's the last of it," Sonata said to me as I dumped my rucksack on the ground with a grunt.

Sonata then pulled out his map case and said, "Here's our situation, Mike. We're approximately here, and by 1600 hours today, they want us here, in the valley."

I couldn't believe what I was hearing. "Christ Almighty Six, that's a mile from here, and it's over a 2,500 foot drop in elevation. We have no idea how many ravines are between us and there, let alone dinks."

"I don't like it either, but we've been placed under the operational control of the 198th Light Infantry Brigade to participate in Operation Wheeler/Wallowa. Apparently, this is going to be a big one and they want us to get to LZ Ross for rest and resupply before it starts. We won't have time for resupply here, so have everyone conserve water until we get there. Get your men ready to move in thirty minutes. You'll lead."

"Roger that, Six." I then turned and spoke with Sgt. Hodges who immediately went to the squad leaders and passed the word. We were ready and moving in fifteen minutes.

On our way down from the mountains to the valley below, we encountered a picturesque, three-meter wide mountain stream tumbling down the side of the ridge. My platoon elements, led by Gates' squad, had already moved through the stream to secure the opposite side. As I arrived at the stream, men were already buried face deep in the cool water and were drinking thirstily as they filled their canteens.

"What the hell are you men doing?" I yelled as I got to the stream bank. "Get your face's outta there and secure the stream above. We don't know what's here. Get your ass moving."

By then, the rest of the platoon has started to bunch up behind me and I signaled a stop.

I then saw Van Artsdalen coming from upstream and heading my way. "LT, I checked all the way up the stream about 100 meters. It's clear. Way too steep for any dinks to be hiding. But there's a problem."

"What's that, Van? What kind of problem?"

"LT, we got a dead dink in the stream, all bloated up, just around that big rock up there," Van Artsdalen said, pointing to a huge boulder that sat mid-stream about fifty meters from our location.

When the men closest to me heard what he said, canteens started emptying and some men looked a little pale. I looked right at them and said, "That'll teach you men from being in a hurry. Get those damn canteens emptied. Sergeant Gates, send half of your squad upstream above the body for security and I'll send the rest of the platoon up there in three's to refill."

"Roger, that, LT."

UNACCOUNTED

I reached over and tapped my radioman, Macintyre, to call Six and tell him the situation.

Thirty minutes later we were moving again. Luckily, we encountered no more surprises as we arrived at the valley floor at 1530 hours. Right on time.

The company was airlifted that afternoon back to LZ Ross and ordered to resupply, rearm and stand-down. We needed some rest. We had held our own on the high ridges of Hill 922, but the engagements had been costly to us. The company was now short two experienced field officers with just two remaining, Captain Sonata and me.

When we off loaded from the choppers and walked into LZ Ross, we looked pretty damn rough. The men were filthy, unshaven, and their jungle uniforms were ripped, torn, and stained by red clay and mud from their time on 922. Green towels hung from some men as scarves. Bandoliers of ammo were slung across each man's chest; grenades flopped on the straps of their ruck. The men were strolling from the choppers heading towards the secure confines of an LZ. Cigarettes hung from their mouths. Weapons were carried casually; magazines still loaded. Bad attitudes still engaged.

We usually didn't see many HQ non-infantry troops when we came into an LZ to stand-down. The hostility and disdain our infantrymen had for troops who never left base camp was open and visceral. The blood ties infantry troops shared isolated them from all other soldiers who were not infantry. The non-infantry types soon learned to avoid us when we first arrived.

Our days of rest at LZ Ross were mixed with some light duty bridge and security work on Highway 535. We were lucky. We didn't endure any casualties and the work was easy.

I knew something big was about to happen when on the afternoon of 3 May, a reporter and photographer from a newspaper in the States showed up at Ross. I was standing by a bunker bullshitting with Sgt. Hodges and Macintyre when they arrived on the afternoon supply slick. After a few minutes they found us.

"Afternoon, men. I'm Rob Cothran and this is Bill Simpson. We're with the San Francisco Chronicle. Can we talk to you men for a few minutes?"

I hadn't seen an American civilian since being in Vietnam, let alone a reporter. Cothran was a tall, beanpole of a man in his early 30s. He had dark hair and a friendly engaging smile. He was wearing a blue, open collar shirt and khaki pants. Simpson, his photographer was short and stocky, and had several cameras hanging from his neck. His blue Detroit Tigers baseball cap was worn tilted back on his head, and he had sunglasses on.

Cothran continued, "We've been over at Chu Lai and the commanders there said if we wanted to see some action to come here or go up north with the 101st Airborne."

Hodges, ever the diplomat responded first, "It's nice to see you gentlemen, but I think you have come to the wrong place. This spot here is the jumping off point to those mountains and hills over there. This is the Que Son. You'd be better off with those boys in the airborne, they are probably used to the press and could take better care of you."

Cothran and Simpson looked at each other and then Cothran asked me. "What about that Lieutenant? What do you think?"

I looked at them both. "Sergeant Hodges is probably right. We're an infantry unit, and most of our work is done on the ground; soon up in those mountains. It's probably the last place you want to be. You'd be just a grunt without a weapon, and we don't have the helicopter support of the 101st. Once you're with us, you'd be stuck."

Cothran and Simpson thanked us for the information, and an hour later they were headed back out to Chu Lai for friendlier locales. I wasn't surprised.

On 4 May 1968, Delta Company was ordered out on Search and Clear operations in the triple canopy and heavily forested hills of the Que Son Valley near LZ Ross. Operation Wheeler/Wallowa had begun in earnest.

Chapter 20

TOO LATE FOR CHARLES

Narrative: *M. McDonald-Low*

2011

I was dreaming again.

I was on my back. I had fallen over the small rock wall that bordered the dry streambed. I looked down at my shoulder and arm, which had swollen grotesquely from the impact of the rounds. I thought it should have been worse given how close he was.

"The dink has bad ammo," I said to myself, as I sat up and reached for my M16, which had been blown out of my hands. Rounds had impacted my weapon above the magazine and just below the ejection port cover and had splintered and ricocheted pieces into my lower arm, but left the M16 still serviceable. Two other rounds had hit me in the shoulder and bicep. The entry wounds had swollen and distorted immediately, but I didn't feel a thing. I picked up my M16 and leaned forward resting the muzzle on the rock wall. And waited.

Sure enough, not ten seconds later, I saw the trap door pop open and those small brown eyes peered out from their darkened hole, looking up trail.

"Too late for you, Charles," I said to myself as I put a short burst into the NVA soldier. The rounds smashed into his face and upper body and pushed him violently back and then down into the hole. The trap door flopped shut.

I waited. No movement. I crawled over the rock wall and stood up holding my 16. I looked back up trail. The real nightmare was just beginning to unfold. I counted three men down as far as I could tell, and it looked like one of Cerutti's two new ammo bearers was dead. Cerutti had been hit as well, but he was already pumping rounds uphill. He paused and looked at me. I pointed up the trail. "Take your 60 and start hammering to the left of the trail, not right. Keep it far left," I yelled.

He stood and started shooting in fifteen-twenty round bursts, the expended casings from his M60 machine gun spitting out in an arc before reaching the ground and the men at his feet. He had slung belts of M60 ammo around his chest, and I could see them sliding across him as he fired.

To my right, Macintyre was just making his way over the rocky wall. He had caught some shrapnel, but looked okay. He carried his helmet and I noticed a big gouge on the left side.

"Almost got me, LT, but I am good to go," he said tossing the helmet to the ground.

"Mac, let's get the other platoons moving forward. We need men to the front and we're gonna' need a Dust Off."

Macintyre looked and me, "Roger, LT. I'm on it."

I looked over Mac's shoulder, and I saw men surging forward up the trail. I told Sgt. Hodges, who had just come up to me, to keep the men spread out and watching their flanks. I also told him we had three men up trail to the left of the "Y" and down trail over the edge. Hodges told me I needed a medic and then started moving up trail past Cpt. Sonata and his RTOs who were coming down from above.

Sonata looked at me and said, "Jesus, Mike you look like shit. You're bleeding everywhere. Thanks for the push, saved my ass." He then looked over his shoulder and yelled for Curtis, the new head medic of the company.

Jeffers, one of the captain's RTOs yelled over at Sonata, "He's not coming, sir. He's up the trail with casualties."

"Six, don't forget I have three guys up trail and three over the top. We're going to need some help up there."

I continued to hear small arms' and machine gun fire, though it sounded more infrequent and more like our weapons and not theirs. Macintyre was unpacking a field dressing and looking at me, "LT, let's get that arm stopped up and your head is bleeding again. Not real good."

Chuck was already on the radio calling for a Dust Off and reporting the situation. Lt. Bennett had just come up, Sonata stopped talking on the radio and told him, "Bennett, get your men to that small opening over there and cut us out an LZ. I've got Dust Off here in one five minutes!"

Bennett turned and yelled at his platoon sergeant pointing to a small flat spot that flared out from the trail and dry streamed to the right. It had a lot of heavy brush and foliage, but no trees. Bennett's men started moving as he and his sergeant pointed and then followed them to where the LZ was to be cut. I heard sporadic gunfire continuing up the trail, but it sounded like ours.

Just then my knees gave out and I was sitting on my ass. I stood back up and thought "weird," but then realized I had a little shock setting in on me. The next fifteen minutes passed as a blur of men, shooting, wounded men suffering, and the constant shouts and orders of Sonata, Hodges and Bennett.

I remembered the Dust Off gently balancing on the small apron Bennett and his men had cut. It looked as if the bird was perched half on and half off a small cliff on the edge of the cleared area. It hovered just barely touching the ground. There was dust from the rotor wash everywhere as men bent to avoid the blades. The two Dust Off crewmen helped the terribly wounded men from my platoon onto the helicopter. I noticed three bodies in the chopper covered in ponchos.

Nelson still had the spring bobbing wildly from his chest as a medic rushed him to the Dust Off.

Sonata grabbed me by my arm and told me, "You're outta here One Six. Good luck." I simply nodded, and a medic grabbed me and guided me on board the Dust Off.

I felt the bird lift off, struggling with the ten casualties on board. We were overloaded. As the slick turned and pushed off the apron, its nose dipped momentarily, then the bird gathered air speed and lifted up into the sky. I remembered looking at the dead and wounded men in the chopper when suddenly I heard a loud bang and the chopper twisted thirty degrees mid-air. It then straightened, dipped, and gathered speed again. I learned later that we had taken a .51 caliber round through our tail, but miraculously it had missed all internal components and passed through the Huey, leaving a fifty-cent sized hole in the fuselage.

The "bang" of the round as it hit the Dust Off woke me from the nightmare. I sat up and took a deep breath. I knew my life and theirs had been forever changed. I remembered I had looked down at the ground as we flew off that hill and headed for LZ Baldy and the forward area treatment center. I had wondered about what would happen to the last men of Delta still on the trail that led to the "Y."

I sighed and stretched. I looked at the clock and it read 0400 hours. Time; it seemed my whole life had been on the clock, and it rarely slowed down. I thought about the two months of hospitals and treatments I had to endure before I saw Delta Company again. By then, everything had changed. When I returned it was as their company commander and it was never reported to me that one man was left behind above the "Y."

My actions and memories of 11 May would not cross my mind again for many years.

Chapter 21

NARROWING THE SEARCH

M. McDonald-Low

2010

EMAIL

Michael McDonald-Low to Carne, Ray Civ JPAC J2

28 Sept 2010

Ray,

After carefully sifting through 1/6 Infantry After-Action Reports of May 11, I have discovered 1/6 Infantry made an error in their reporting.

"At 1148 hours Alpha Company 1-6 Infantry has made contact at 065254, have 2 WHA at 067253, received automatic weapons and small arms fire. They were able to recover 2 of the three bodies, Delta Company 1-6 Infantry." Note that in this AAR they have misidentified the unit. D 1/6 Infantry was not at this location. It was D 1/20.

A1/6 had moved down the ridgeline to their reported positions. It indicates that between my coordinates and theirs is the location of 1165. Again, on site exploration will help pinpoint the locale exactly.

Will we have permission to also work down from hill 348 (LZ Center)?

Michael

———

EMAIL

Carne, Ray Civ JPAC J2 to Michael McDonald-Low

28 Sept 2010

Michael,

We can do whatever we want; we just have to pay for it. This is when our investigation becomes a frustrating factor. I have to be so precise with my lead requirements because they will budget everything meter by meter.

Ray

———

EMAIL

Michael McDonald-Low to Carne, Ray Civ JPAC J2, cc: Holmes, Catherine Capt. USAF

30 Oct 2010

Dear Ray & Catherine,

Hope this finds you both well.

I have just finished reviewing the daily logs from 1/6 Infantry and I have determined I have made a slight error on exact locations.

I wanted to bring it to your attention as soon as I discovered it and verified the information. I have. It will slightly affect our trail walk and search request. Please refer to the map below for the coordinates. I have sent it previously.

"At 0645 hours, D/1-20 departed their NDP location BT083247, heading north and across the valley through a small village. D/1-20 headed up out of the valley at BT076250 following an old streambed and trail. D/1-20 followed the streambed north as it meandered to where it reached the top of the ridgeline at BT070258 at a trail intersection. At 0840 hours 1st Platoon elements of D/1-20 come under heavy machine gun fire up trail from BT070258."

This information definitely helps to closer pinpoint 1165.

Michael McDonald-Low

Chapter 22

RUNNING TOWARDS TROUBLE

Narrative: *Lt. McDonald-Low*

5 May 1968

We had continued our clearing operations around the foothills just north of LZ Ross on 4 May. Early in the morning of 5 May, at approximately 0300 hours, we watched from our night defensive position and saw LZ Ross get pounded with 122mm rockets and mortars. On the battalion net, I listened to the radio traffic and the incoming casualty reports. Calls for Dust Off indicated they had nine wounded. It was proving to be a kick-off for a terrible day in the Que Son. Macintyre kept me updated on the PRC-25 and reported their Dust Off at Ross was completed at 0747 hours.

"Delta One Six, this is Six, over." It was Sonata.

Macintyre passed me the handset, "One Six, go."

"One Six, I have just received an emergency transmission from 1/6 Infantry. Let's pull back to that flat spot, where we started yesterday. Secure an LZ so we can get ready to CA out of here. Make it big enough for three birds per lift. Apparently a slick and a gunship have been shot down over near LZ Center and they want us there ASAP."

"Roger that."

Sgt. Hodges had been listening and was already moving toward the squads' positions along the trail. I could hear him shouting to the squads, "We're gonna saddle up, turn 180 and head back to the flats, but let's not get sloppy."

I checked my maps as the platoon turned an about face and headed back down to the paddies and grasses of the flats below. The other platoons of Delta had already begun their migrations as well, each moving down trail from their own search locations. Sonata and the HQ were moving with 3rd Platoon.

After an uneventful and relatively quick trek back to the grass lands, the company had fanned out waiting for our ride out. I soon learned the details on the shoot downs. At 1030 hours a "Minuteman" slick from the 176th AHC was shot down in the valley, southeast of LZ Center at coordinates BT072245. At 1045 hours, a covering "Firebird" gunship from the 71st AHC was also shot down right next to the slick at BT075248. Large NVA troop movements were observed under way throughout the AO around LZ Center.

It was 1330 hours. Six had already informed me that I was going on the first bird and I was to establish contact with Bravo Company, 1/6 Infantry who were already on site.

As we waited for the slicks, I heard more details on the battalion radio net describing the shot down slick as carrying a four-man long-range reconnaissance patrol (LRRP) identified as LRRP "Rosie." Soldiers from B/1-6 had combat air assaulted at 1435 hours to secure the area near the downed aircraft. The company commander of B/1-6, Kansas Six, reported at 1544 hours that seven KIA, three MIA, and four WIA were at the two helicopter crash sites. There was negative contact with the enemy, but numerous reports of NVA troop movements were coming in from Helix 25, an Air Force forward air controller who was on station in the area.

At 1728 hours, I was the first of ninety-six soldiers of D/1-20 to land at BT073247, in the heart of the Que Son Valley.

Note: The 3rd Regiment of the 2nd NVA Division supported by the 1st VC Regiment made its first attack on LZ Center in the heart of the Que Son Valley on May 5, 1968 the beginning of their "mini-Tet" offensive and the Americal Division's Operation Wheeler/Wallowa.

The Que Son Valley AO fell under the overall jurisdiction of the 2nd NVA Division and its 3rd NVA Regiment, which was now commanded by an officer named in North Vietnamese Army documents as Cao Niem. The 3rd NVA Regiment's mission was to annihilate the current residents of LZ Center, the 198th Light Infantry Brigade's 1-6th Infantry battalion. A second part of its mission was to inflict extreme casualties on any other Allied reinforcements that would arrive to help. Strengthened with a sapper battalion (minus one company), a 12.7mm anti-aircraft company, and one 82mm mortar company, about 950 men in total, the 3rd Regiment was a daunting force. Also bolstering the regiment was over 900 local and main force troops of the 1st Viet Cong Regiment; men that grew up the valley and were extremely familiar with its surrounding hills.

The NVA commander, Cao Niem, believed that success hinged on controlling the high ground around LZ Center, and he had arrayed three infantry battalions around several hilltop strongpoints. The cornerstone of the regiments plan was a bastion on the grassy ridge of Nui Hoac (Hill 352) that defended at least two anti-aircraft guns some 2,500 meters south of LZ Center. The number of NVA soldiers who held the Nui Hoac position is unknown, but it was a substantial force supported by mortars, heavy and light machine guns, and recoilless rifles. It was also backed up by a strong reserve armed with automatic weapons, typically AK-47's.* From *Through the Valley: Vietnam, 1967-1968* by James F. Humphries. Copyright © 1999 by Lynne Rienner Publishers. Used with permission of the publisher.

Chapter 23

BIRDS ON THE GROUND

Narrative: *Lt. McDonald-Low*

5 May 1968

As we flew towards our insertion point, our three lead slicks were joined by two Firebird gunships. We were all flying a circuitous route heading first west and then south around LZ Center. While we were still at altitude, I could see the Que Son Valley as it stretched from the dark green mountains of Hiep Duc towards LZ Center and the heart of the valley. Along the valley floor I could see the skeletal remains of several jets, their buried tails standing like tombstones along the edge of the mountains.

As the choppers banked left to approach our LZ, we sharply dropped to come up the valley low and fast at about 100 feet off the deck. I could see hooches spread out along the edge of the paddies, forming a large thumbprint on the valley floor.

Our Firebird gunship escorts were now rotating mini-gun fire and rockets into a steep ridgeline 500 meters north of the

LZ and along the edge of paddies bordering the hills that rose green and deadly from the floor. At the very edge of the flooded paddies, bamboo and elephant ears grew along the banks next to where dense trees and underbrush led up the steep hills. Smoke hung around the edges of the paddies and two white plumes of dense smoke were rising from the nearby jungle. I observed many soldiers of Bravo Company, 1/6 Infantry spread out along the south end of the paddies next to the tree line and along the east end where I assumed the downed helicopters were located. I could also see another group of grunts off to the southwest.

Our bird raced in and flared its nose and the door gunner and crew chief started yelling, "Go. Go. Go."

Sgt. Gates, Van Artsdalen, Clay, Lockhart, my RTO Macintyre, and myself jumped out of our slick into the paddy. The water was about eighteen inches deep. We all ducked as the chopper pulled away, its nose just above the paddy. As we slogged for the edge of the paddy to get out of the water and mud, I could see four infantrymen had paused to watch us from the raised dike of the paddy wall.

As I crawled up and over the wall of the paddy, the three quickly spotted my blacked out LT bar and identified themselves as soldiers of Bravo Company, 1/6 Infantry. The infantrymen were carrying a poncho between them, and it was filled with dismembered legs and feet. I had become somewhat insensitive to death and gross wounds, but the sight of those six or seven legs all bent at different angles, and some still wearing mangled jungle trousers and boots, was an insane show-stopper.

With no explanation of their gruesome cargo, one of the soldiers told me, "This is a really bad area LT. My Six, Kansas Six, is just up this trail over in that brushy area and they're working the crash site. He says to come on up to his location. We have both dead and wounded we're working with." Pointing south and west he said, "Over there is where the rest of the company is. Our Two Six and Three Six elements are patrolling for some NVA that were spotted by a forward air controller about ten minutes ago."

Over his shoulder, I saw intense white smoke billowing up out of the canopy pinpointing the burning wreckage of the downed helicopters. Dull white flames were licking skyward as the hulls of both choppers had now fully ignited.

I headed to the crash sites as another lift of three slicks nosily flared into the paddy depositing eighteen more heavily laden infantrymen of Delta. Forty minutes later, the sixth lift containing Captain Sonata and the rest of the Company HQ arrived. When I saw him land, I went over and greeted him and then escorted him to the burning choppers and Kansas Six, Bravo Company's CO, Captain Jim Abrason.

I briefed Sonata on what I knew as we walked over to meet up with Captain Abrason. "The choppers are totally 86'ed. I did not see any survivors, but there's still a lot of activity going on. It was not good. Kansas Six has told me the big deal here is the NVA are under movement everywhere and control all of the high ground. It's been tough to get birds in because of all the NVA anti-aircraft guns positioned on the hilltops. They're shooting down on any aircraft that come into the valley. They're also using some .51 caliber machine guns and 82mm mortars."

The thump, thump, thump of mortar fire suddenly invaded my conversation with Chuck and I heard someone yell, "Incoming!" Everyone dove for the ground. "Perfect timing," I thought to myself as I hugged the ground.

The enemy had apparently observed our combat assault and link-up with Bravo Company because we started receiving a mix of 60mm and 82mm mortar rounds just as our final troops dropped in at the LZ.

As we lay side by side, Chuck grabbed the handset from his RTO, Jim Daley. Just as he did he looked over at me and asked, "Where do you think the mortars are shooting from?"

I pulled my map case out of my thigh pocket and set it flat in front of me. "I mark our location at BT083275. My best guess is that the mortars are at BT083242."

Chuck nodded at me and called Kansas Six, "Kansas Six, this is Delta Six. I'm going to get some air help. We've got a Helix overhead and he can kill that mortar fire for us."

"Roger that, Delta Six. We'll keep our heads down."

Sonata then called Helix Two Five, an Air Force forward air controller who was circling the area on station. "Helix Two Five, Helix Two Five, this is Crossbow Delta Six, over."

"Helix Two Five, go ahead."

"We'd like to request an immediate air strike at coordinates BT083242. We are receiving mortar fire from that location, over."

"Delta Six, you're in luck. I've got a couple of Phantom fast movers on station, just zero three minutes out with a load of 250s. Please pop smoke to ID your locations, over."

"Delta Six, roger that." I was close enough to Sonata to hear the transmissions and rolled over on my back, grabbed a smoke grenade off my web belt, and rolled back. I heaved it thirty feet to the front.

"Helix Two Five, we have popped smoke at our location. Please identify, over."

"Delta Six, gotcha yellow smoke, over."

"Roger, Helix. Be advised we have Kansas Six with us at our locale and we occupy the area circling the small hill to the east. Our smoke is almost dead center on our locations. Enemy troops to our south and west, over."

"Helix, roger. Phantoms two minutes out. Dig in, it's going to be close."

As the strike came in, we looked up and observed large NVA weapons firing at the two jets from Nui Hoac Ridge and an adjacent hill just east of LZ Center. It looked like anti-aircraft and .51 caliber fire.

The 250 pounders then landed and the concussions were huge. The ground jumped when they hit, and I could feel myself being lifted off the ground. It was deafening, and the shock wave seemed to flatten everything. Then it was totally quiet.

The silence was broken when I heard someone yelling, "Medic!" and GIs were soon shouting and moving all around me. I listened to the battalion net, and I could hear Kansas Six requesting a Dust Off for three B/1-6 soldiers who were injured from the air strike. As I listened, Captain Sonata started talking with Abrason and they agreed to establish and consolidate their positions on a small hill and ridge about 500 meters east of us. Five minutes later, both companies were on the move before more mortar fire could be directed at us. Twenty minutes later we arrived on our side of the hill.

"I'm going to establish my HQ over near that rocky out cropping," Sonata said to me, pointing to a small clearing with large boulders about fifty feet away. "Spread your platoon down and around on the edge where we came up.

2nd and 3rd Platoon's will be on your left and right linking around to Bravo Company. Make sure you're tight."

Not thirty seconds later, as I had begun moving my platoon with Sgt. Hodges, I heard a small boom. I thought it was a mortar when I heard soldiers yelling, "Incoming! Incoming!"

We all listened, but there were no other telltale thumps of a mortar. I got up from my prone position and headed back to where I had last seen Chuck. I could see a small haze of smoke by his position and I could smell the ozone. Sonata was standing and yelling on the radio with his RTO next to him, there were men down everywhere around him.

"This is Crossbow Delta Six, request immediate Dust Off at my location, over."

I heard the radio static, a pause and then, "Roger that, Delta Six. Verify coordinates as we have a Dust Off on the way, over."

Sonata looked at me and waved me over. I looked at the map that I had just pulled from my thigh pocket as I walked over to him. I then pointed to it and told him the coordinates, which he then repeated to Dust Off Control.

I could see that the damage was pretty severe. I counted seven GIs down and spread out around him, all suffering from multiple shrapnel wounds. Hank Kotsaris, the company's head medic was dead, his right arm and leg blown off. Medics from nearby B Company were already running towards us to help.

Chuck dropped the radio handset, turned and yelled at me, apparently still somewhat deaf from the explosion. "It was a 'Bouncing Betty' mine! There was no mortar fire. Can you believe it, One Six? A goddamn French mine, probably been here since '52. Daley and I were shielded by Kotsaris and the other men who were behind him. Apparently, Kotsaris stepped on the old mine and triggered it. It popped up five feet into the air before it exploded."

At 1730 hours, Sonata reported to our command, 1-6 Infantry, that we had sustained one KIA and six WIA. All were dusted off uneventfully, just as night fell.

Chapter 24

NOTHIN' BUT DEAD GUYS

Narrative: *Spec. 4 Clifford Van Artsdalen*

5 May 1968

When I heard the "boom," I knew it wasn't going to be good. When the LT got back, he told us that it was an old French mine, a "Bouncing Betty," and seven men were down with a Dust Off chopper on the way. That left us shorthanded because I knew that the HQ guys were going to be replaced by riflemen from each platoon and one platoon was also going to lose a medic. As it was, we only had about eighty infantrymen spread throughout the three platoons. In 1st Platoon we had twenty-six, and in my squad there were just eight: Gates, Roosevelt, Cerutti, Jackson, Milner, Zapata, Big Todd, and me.

We were digging in on a small, raised finger of land just above the valley floor as it began to turn to dusk. B Company, 1/6 Infantry, and ours were in a night defensive perimeter together. I guess Delta Six and Kansas Six had thought it best to have safety in numbers this night. The high ridge of Nui

Hoac loomed above us, and I could also see across to the other side of the valley to the upper ridge of where LZ Center was located. Smoke from the downed choppers drifted in the valley, white and lazy above their doomed locations. We had heard everyone on board was dead, including the LRRP team.

Lost in thought, I had stopped digging my fighting pit when Roosevelt tapped me on the shoulder and said, "Van, I got a real bad feeling about this place. Nothin' but dead guys all around here. Look at where we are, in the middle of fuckin' nowhere. That big mother fuckin' hill up there, you can bet the dinks are all over that place. They shoot at jets, choppers, anything flyin'. Those bitches ain't afraid! Ain't no big thang, but this sucks big time. I don't like it one bit."

I was surprised. I had never heard Roosevelt be fearful of anything or sound unsure. Like all of us grunts, he didn't want to die, but he never said anything about it.

"Roosevelt, just remember you are the man. Nobody has the balls to fuck with you. This ain't no big thang. Hell, we kicked their ass on 922, just gonna' be another repeat here. Rack'em and stack'em," I said, almost believing it myself.

Todd Lockhart, who had been listening from the next fighting pit over said in that easy drawl of his, "My, my. Just listen to you boys. Talkin' shit all the time about dink's never standing and fightin'. Well boys, y'all got your wish. They are sure nuff here to scrap with us. Keep your heads down deep tonight, my ladies, and wrap up tight in y'all's warm and snugglies. The shit will hit the fan tomorrow, boy."

We all believed what Big Todd had to say, but it didn't make anyone feel better hearing it said aloud. The night of 5 May closed without further incident for us although at LZ Center, just uphill from our valley position, the action continued unabated. That night the NVA attacked the perimeter of LZ Center at the steepest part of the ridgeline. It all began at about 0050 hours. Roosevelt leaned over and whispered to me, "Someone is catching hell, Van. I'm sure glad it ain't us. Those mother fuckers are hittin' the bunkers up there, you can bet, just look."

We looked up towards LZ Center, and we could see parachute flares drifting over the firebase and the flash of sporadic small arms' fire accompanying the deep, bass thumping of rockets impacting the base. Moments later you would hear the larger booms of American artillery howitzers returning fire. We couldn't see or hear more than that, but we knew it was serious and deadly.

"It looks like a regular party up there, Roosevelt, but I'm glad we're not invited. They're dancing on the wire tonight. You can bank that, my man," I said quietly to him.

Lockhart, who was dug in with Roosevelt and me, captured it all when he said tugging at my sleeve, "To tell you the truth, Van Artsdalen, better them than us, boy. We got no barbwire. No bunkers. No artillery. No hot chow. No cold beer. No nothin'. Let them party tonight with Charles."

Zapata, in the next fighting pit over, chimed in a loud whisper, "I think you got it right, Texas. Let them rear echelon mutha' fucka's deal with the dinks tonight. If I had that much firepower, I'd own this valley, homeys. Fuck this shit."

Sgt. Hodges must have heard us because in the next moment he was sliding into our fighting pit and stepping on Lockhart who was trying to curl up in his poncho liner.

"Ouch! Jesus, Sarge, what's up?"

"I have been listening to you men for the past ten minutes and I want to remind you all to stay focused on your job. Be calm. The extraneous comments do not impress me and frankly they make the new men concerned. So keep your shit together and pipe down," Hodges said sternly, and then just as quickly slid out of our pit and continued down the line. I assumed he was spreading the word.

I looked over at Clay, leaned into him and in a really low whisper I said, "Sgt. Hodges has the biggest balls I have ever seen on a man. I don't even think the guy sweats. Man of fuckin' steel."

Roosevelt just nodded, clearly afraid to have Hodges hear us.

UNACCOUNTED

We all hunkered down. The night passed slowly in two-hour intervals as we each took turns trying to sleep. I didn't. I kept thinking about what Roosevelt had said. It gave me the willies. I tried not to think about it, but I did. It was like an itch I couldn't scratch, and I didn't like it.

I kept my hand on my M79 all night.

Chapter 25

INDIAN COUNTRY

Narrative: *Lt. McDonald-Low*

6 May 1968

After-Action Report: LZ Center... At 0105 hours, 6 May , two North Vietnamese (NVA) soldiers penetrated the perimeter and trip flares were ignited in the wire. At 0330 hours, ten NVA 122-mm rockets launched from BT990265 impacted on the firebase. At 0440 hours, Bunkers #8 & #9 engaged 4 NVA soldiers with M79 grenade rounds. At 0941 hours, a CH-47 Chinook Boxcar resupply chopper from the 178th ASHC was fired on by an NVA rocket propelled grenade while trying to land at the firebase. An additional suspect enemy mortar site was pinpointed at BT055225. At 1004 hours, an NVA rocket-launching site was spotted by an aerial observer at BT265076.

The ground attacks at LZ Center on 5 and 6 May 1968, resulted in 18 NVA soldiers killed, and the capture of 8 AK-47 rifles, 5 rocket propelled grenade launchers, and one 9-mm pistol. Documents taken from the body of an NVA officer identified the attacking forces as elements of the 3rd NVA Regiment, 2nd NVA Division.

At 0500 hours, I woke up to a soft drizzle and my poncho liner soaked. I was warm and dreaming of somewhere else; someplace dry with a beach and blue water.

"Morning LT," Macintyre said to me as he passed me an aluminum canteen cup filled with hot coffee. As a radioman, Mac was about as good as they came.

I stretched and reached for the cup. My dreams were over; it was time to start another day. "Give me a situation report, Mac."

"Good to see you too, Sir," Macintyre said in that voice that meant he really did and didn't mean it. "Shit hole, in a nutshell LT. We're going to be in it up to our fucking elbows pretty soon. LZ Center had rockets most of the night, and they almost shot down a Chinook. These guys want to rock with us. Our line is good and no reports of any contact."

To tell you the truth, I knew the quiet wouldn't last long. The enemy was here to fight, not run. The platoon was ready, I felt. Although there were only twenty-six of them, all except five newbies could handle themselves in combat. Mac knew his shit, and by then, I trusted him with my thoughts.

"Mac, there is no doubt we're going to find and engage the NVA here. Look around. I would be here if I were them. Really good Indian country."

"Roger that, LT. Should I have Sergeant Hodges rally the men?"

"Absolutely. I'm ready," I said, rising to my feet, dumping the remains of the grounds that had accumulated in the cup. I shrugged, reached down and stuffed my poncho liner into my rucksack. I belted on my pistol belt with its .45 caliber pistol and six ammo pouches stuffed with M16 magazines. I slipped on another bandolier of magazines around my neck and shoulder. I picked up my rucksack and threw it on my back. The nylon shoulder straps' pads and back strap of the aluminum frame and pack settled heavily onto my collarbones and hips. I grabbed my M16, and patted my right thigh just to make sure I felt the maps safe and secure in their polyurethane casing.

It was an easy night, as we had no ambush patrols. Everyone stayed inside the dual company laager, and no one complained.

Mac was on the radio and giving squad leaders a heads-up as Sgt. Hodges walked up to me and said, "LT, I have checked the men, walked the perimeter, and all is good. The men are collecting their gear and getting ready to go."

"Thank you, Sergeant Hodges. Let's get under way in the next few minutes," I said, shaking a cigarette from its pack. I offered Sgt. Hodges one, but he shook his head preferring his non-filtered Camels.

A single-shot sniper round then slammed into the front of our position and we all hit the ground.

I looked toward Delta Six. I could see him busy on the radios with the FO. The new artillery forward observer assigned to us, Lt. Morgan, was pointing at a position to the northwest of us as he shook his map and talked into the radio handset. He looked shook up. I listened to him on the radio.

"Roger, Red Leg Two Six, this is Red Leg Foxtrot Oscar One Six. Mark coordinates BT070239. Request smoke, over."

"Roger that Red Leg Two Six, smoke on the way."

Three more single shots then banged in close to our perimeter. Everyone was down near their half-filled fighting pits.

I reached into my pocket, pulled my map out and checked the coordinates. I was pleasantly surprised to see he was damn close.

The sniper shot had originated from the upper base of Nui Hoac Ridge. As I looked at the target area, I saw white smoke as the smoke round slammed into the hill with a dull thud. "Shit, he's short of where it should be," I said to no one in particular.

I heard Morgan call in again, "Red Leg Two Six, this is Red Leg Foxtrot Oscar One Six. Up five zero, two rounds HE, over."

Hodges was listening, too. "LT, he's damn confident firing high explosive rounds after only one smoke for targeting."

Thirty seconds later we listened to the HE rounds whistling in and then the louder concussions of their high explosive loads. They were a lot closer to our position than I would have wanted. Mac thought so, too. "Holy crap, LT. That's on our right flank of the company. He is very short."

Just then we heard the call for "Medic!" and realized it must have been close to 2nd Platoon's position.

I heard Morgan yelling into his handset to make an adjustment. "Red Leg Two Six, this is Red Leg Foxtrot Oscar One Six. Up 100, right 50. Request air and ground burst. Fire for effect, over."

"Everybody keep your heads down, here comes the big stuff!" I heard Hodges shouting to the left and right.

Twenty seconds later, five shells slammed successively into the base of Nui Hoac Ridge and Hill 352 with violent concussions. I felt the punch as the rounds crushed the hillsides vegetation. Dull, blackish gray smoke from five points of impact circled above the area where we suspected the sniper. Twenty seconds later, another five rounds burst ugly mushrooms above the same circle. The air burst had pelted the entire area with vicious shrapnel and concussion.

It was silent. You could have heard a pin drop.

As if in defiance to the artillery strike, a burst of AK fire, coupled with three rapidly fired sniper rounds, raked our company position. All of the rounds were high and poorly aimed, but it didn't keep anyone from ducking.

"Goddammit, you can bet those dinks are running back to their base. That was just a probe to get our attention," Sonata said to me as he walked up to where I now stood with Mac, Hodges, and Nelson.

As company commander, Sonata always liked postulating about the current condition of the shit we were facing. He pulled out his map and said to me, "2nd Platoon took some shrapnel, but no real damage. Walking wounded, so we're good. I just got a call from the Big Six, and they want us to Recon in force a route up 352, but first we'll look into the success of that arty strike and those snipers. We'll go across that paddy there and check access up that draw," he said, pointing at the paddy and then the map.

"You'll lead, but when we get to the paddy we'll cross it with platoons on line, staggered by squads. Wait for 2nd and 3rd Platoon to get up on your flanks. Let's mount up in one zero minutes."

"Roger that, Six," I responded, checking my map.

I turned to Hodges and Mac, "Let's get the word out and get ready to go. Send Sergeant Gates over. I want his squad on point."

Twenty minutes later we were on the edge of a rice paddy. Dense brush was behind us and across the paddy. Several straw and mud huts sat near the edge of the paddy dike about 250 meters away. Phu Lam 2 was the name of the small ville' on my map. Smoke from a fire pit in the village had cast a fog like shroud through the ville'. The ville' looked deserted, but they usually did in this area. 2nd and 3rd Platoons had spread out on the right and left. Captain Sonata had joined me and given the word to head out. Gates and his squad led our platoon as we began our movement across the open paddy. I felt that we were very exposed.

We were nearly halfway across the brown watered paddy when the first AK47 opened up. The rounds danced across the water in front of the lead squads. Everyone hit the deck and those in front began returning fire. A second and third AK47 rattled at our left and right flanks from behind the hooches in the village. The water was jumping from the rounds.

"Sergeant Gates, get the rest of your squad up on line. Sergeant Hodges move 3rd Squad up and get the M60s going. Let's move it!" I shouted, as Clay, Van Artsdalen, and Lockhart laid down steady fire with other squad elements on their left and right.

Cerutti, our M60 machine gunner, ran past me heading to the front with his ammo bearers running next to him, their ammo cans of belted 7.62 clattering with each step. "Good men," I thought.

I then heard men shouting at each other between bursts of enemy fire as they moved ahead. Above all that noise and gunfire I heard a scream ring out from somewhere on our left flank, "Leeches!"

Not two seconds later two other men screamed at the top of their lungs, "Leeches! They're fucking everywhere."

All of a sudden I saw men stand up all across the paddy and begin shedding their rucksacks, canteens, ammo bandoliers, and jungle shirts. Others had begun shooting and running towards the ville', not waiting for any orders to move ahead.

I couldn't believe my eyes. It took a scant forty-five seconds for the company to secure that village. The men were fearless in the face of the AK47 fire and miraculously no one had been hit. On the paddy shore several men had dropped their gear and weapons and had begun to strip down to their undershorts. The men cursed as they used cigarettes and mosquito repellant to remove the many engorged, brown leeches attached to their bodies. The swearing was caustic, crude, and non-stop.

Gates and elements of his squad along with 3rd Squad had been focused enough to set a perimeter encircling the village. They were now scrutinizing themselves for the bloodsuckers, but most were still on high alert. As I approached the center of the small village, I saw that there were eight or ten hooches that made up the entire village of Phu Lam 2.

Mac had come up next to me listening to his radio handset. I heard the static and voices coming in from Delta Six. "At 1000 hours, forward air controller Helix 25 reported an enemy platoon sized unit moving on the ground near Hill 352. Artillery is being fired at the target and jets are inbound. B/1-6 has reported finding bodies, rucksacks, lighters, wallets, and dog tags at the site of the burned aircraft they secured the day before."

As I listened, fire from AKs banged into our position distantly from the upper heights of 352. I heard several men on our outer perimeter return fire.

"Sergeant Hodges, this area is wide open for trouble. Let's move 2nd and 3rd up with Gates and nail down the ravine going uphill there. I don't want any more fire raining down on us."

Hodges turned and yelled at 2nd and 3rd Squads and they were soon moving up to join Gates' men.

As I moved with my platoon up the hill I heard a muffled explosion go off from the rear of the village. I then heard the call for "Medic!" shouted out. A soldier from 3rd Platoon, a fucking new guy, had decided to clear one of the hooches with a grenade, just like in the movies. He pulled the pin, threw it in through the door and then put his back against the outside wall of the hooch. When the grenade exploded he was peppered with shrapnel that exploded through the mud and straw walls.

"You cannot fix stupid," I thought to myself.

At 1130 hours we dusted off one FNG wounded with grenade frags.

After-Action Report: The presence of two infantry companies on the ground did not deter the NVA. The enemy was brazen in their movement in the area. At 1140 hours, an air strike at BT056276 resulted in a secondary explosion. The jet took automatic weapons fire from NVA while making its bomb run.

In spite of air strikes and artillery attacks, the enemy forces continued to pound LZ Center with mortar fire. At 1350 hours, B/1-6 engaged NVA soldiers in the open at BT087244 resulting in one NVA KIA. At 1400 hours, the Tactical Operations Center at LZ Center suffered a direct hit from two 82-mm rounds, resulting in 7 wounded. At 1800 hours, four more mortar rounds impacted from suspect locations about 1200 meters northwest of the firebase. By 1850 hours, a total of 25 rounds had impacted LZ Center.

Chapter 26

PUFF AND THE PHANTOMS
Narrative: *Spec. 4 Clifford Van Artsdalen*
6 May 1968

Roosevelt, Jackson, and I were on either side of the M60 manned by Cerutti. Cerutti had his machine gun positioned flanking the small trail that extended up into the dense jungle of Hill 352. Daylight was barely filtering in at 1400 hours, and it left the whole place gloomy and shadowed.

We had taken sporadic AK fire from above us all morning, and it had begun again. Cerutti leaned into the M60 and pumped a burst of thirty rounds uphill. The AK fire stopped. We all scrunched down into the dirt and underbrush, trying to blend in. It wasn't difficult, as we were in our normal "be one with the jungle" mode. Our jungle fatigues were sweat soaked, caked with mud, and downright filthy. We hadn't shaved or washed and we all had dirt and remnants of camo stick on our faces. We smelled as bad as we looked, just like the assholes up the hill, the NVA. Everyone on both sides just wanted to be part of the scenery, thus reducing the risk of being an easy target.

At about 1600 hours, the LT pulled us back down off the hillside and we returned to where we had spent the night before with Bravo Company. I was glad to be off 352, but I knew we hadn't even begun to get to the top of that monster. It was quiet when we settled into our night defensive position with Bravo.

At 1705 hours, just before it started to turn to dusk, a "Minuteman" slick touched down inside our perimeter and delivered much needed ammo and water to both companies. Delta also received two new LTs to head up our 2nd and 3rd Platoons. 1st Lt. Wayne Vinson, who was brand-new with thirty-five days in country, got the 2nd, while 1st Lt. Charles Bennett, also new, took over the 3rd. I was just glad they weren't coming to us. New LTs were a real pain in the ass and didn't know shit. They were the worst kind of FNG; they weren't even riflemen.

Over the next hour we dug in our fighting positions and setup Claymore mines and trip flares about twenty yards outside our pit. Sgt. Hodges and the LT had checked our fields of fire, and it was chow time.

It had just turned completely dark as we finished our meals, when a flashing strobe light went off over by the headquarters location of Bravo Company. It was so bright it illuminated our entire perimeter with each flash.

"What the fuck," had barely gotten out of my mouth when I heard the LT say, "Everyone find a hole. We've got 'Puff the Magic Dragon' gunship coming in along with some F-4s who are going to drop some CBU cluster bomb rain on 352 tonight."

We all knew combat at night was quite a visual display. Their tracers were green while ours were red in color. Their muzzle flashes appeared white while ours were yellow. I wasn't prepared for the color show that was to come.

When I saw the big C-124 airplane let go of its first volley of mini-gun fire, I found it hard to believe that anybody could live through all that carnage. The rounds from "Puff" appeared to be a stream of red flowing down from the belly of the 124 and waving on the ground. Every tenth round was a tracer, so I knew the number of rounds actually impacting was huge. The other weirdness of "Puff" and its high-powered rates of firing was the sound. "Puff" seemed to hum and growl when it let go of all those mini-guns. It was easy to see why it had been named "the Magic Dragon," but the NVA weren't spooked. After about a minute of mini-gun fire from "Puff," I watched green NVA tracers from something big reach up and follow "Puff" in the air until it drove them out of the area.

The Air Force wasn't done yet, as two F-4 Phantoms brought in their CBU cluster bomb packages and laid waste to the eastern flank of Hill 352 to quiet the big NVA gun. It was a real spectacle. We could barely see the jets as they made their approach, but then they would slow, drop their tail slightly and then thousands of small white flashbulbs would spray across the ground. The rapid-fire concussions rocked the ridge, briefly illuminating the planes as they roared off into the night with their afterburners glowing. Each of those flashbulbs was the light from a grenade-sized cluster bomb going off, spraying metal everywhere.

We loved "Puff" and the Phantoms that night. Everyone felt more secure and the shit talk about how we were "gonna kick some NVA ass" tomorrow continued into the night. We no longer felt so alone or worried.

Chapter 27

OUTGUNNED

Narrative: *Lt. McDonald-Low*

7 May 1968

After-Action Report: At 0010 hours, B/1-6 received 26 82-mm mortar rounds. At 0100 hours, D/1-20 received 3-4 mortar rounds that fell short 400 meters outside their perimeter with negative results. At 0715 hours, B/1-6 received 6-7 NVA sniper rounds and responded with artillery, which was followed by 10 more sniper rounds from an area around BT070239.

At 0842 hours, D/1-20 received small arms' and automatic fire from BT075233 and sniper fire from BT080238. At 0842 hours, a 71st AHC Firebird gunship was called on station to support D/1-20 as they departed the area due to intense NVA automatic weapons' fire from BT068227. At 0936 hours, forward air controller Helix 25 reports the jet fighters on an air strike in the valley received heavy small arms and automatic weapons fire.

At 1000 hours, forward air controller Helix 25 spotted an enemy platoon sized unit moving on the ground. Artillery was fired at the target until additional jets arrived. At 1025 hours,

one of the A-4 jets from the air strike at BT076226 took a
12.7mm AA hit in his wing tank and broke station to return to
Chu Lai base where he made a successful forced landing.

Our morning began with NVA mortar fire landing just outside our position, and it was soon accompanied by automatic weapons' fire and sniper fire from the base and upper reaches of the ridge. It temporarily pinned us down and we needed gunship support so we could depart our perimeter. As soon as the gunships arrived they came under intense enemy fire, but it gave us enough time to hastily evacuate our position and return to the village across from the paddy that led up to Hill 352. As we began our search of the ville', I sent three men from 3rd Squad fifty meters up an animal trail that climbed towards the top of Hill 352. My intention was to ensure we weren't pelted with any more gunfire from above our position, and for them to also scout the immediate area for any obvious NVA trails.

I then heard the sound of an aircraft and turned to watch a Sky Raider make its bomb run in support of Bravo Company who was beginning their climb up Nui Hoac to our west. Just as the plane dropped its bombs, I observed it take a big hit from something powerful. The prop driven Sky Raider started smoking immediately and I watched him lift skyward and hard over the top of 352.

I was impressed that the NVA were so fearless in taking shots at fighter aircraft. It rarely happened in our previous ops, as it typically brought an immediate and deadly response to the shooters. It was an entirely different story here as they felt they had the upper hand. I soon found out why when I heard Kansas Six on the battalion net, "Situation report for 1155 hours. We have identified five enemy .51 caliber anti-aircraft positions, coordinates follow: BT068227, BT070225, BT074226, BT974224, and BT075225. At 1215 hours, we have also observed an A-1 Sky Raider aircraft exploding after taking hits in the wing section. The aircraft was shot down near BT070225, but the pilot was observed to have bailed out."

After-Action Report: At 1300 hours, when the air strike was completed, mortars, 155-mm and 175-mm artillery were fired from LZ Center into the identified anti-aircraft positions. Intensive anti-aircraft fire in the area, and later the capture of a 12.7mm AA gun, indicated that the enemy's GK-31 AA Battalion had been attached to, or was operating in support of the 3rd NVA Regiment.

It wasn't long after listening to the report by Kansas Six, and then listening to the artillery barrage, that we soon had new orders: reach the top of Hill 352. It was 1300 hours, early afternoon, and it was blazing hot and humid. As we made our climb we received sporadic AK fire that slowed us down, but little else. At about 1435 hours we received several rounds of sniper fire and I heard mortars thumping out from our front. Their impacts were distant to the west and muffled by the terrain we were moving through.

It took us more than two careful hours to reach a small, grassy clearing at the fringe of the top of 352. When I arrived I could see a rocky out cropping about twenty-five meters to our front. I told Gates and his squad to drop their rucksacks and join me at the rocks ahead. We moved to, and then hunkered down behind the rocks as Hodges brought up the remainder of the platoon. It wasn't long before Delta Six joined me after directing 2nd and 3rd Platoons to spread out to our right along the rocks that ran west.

I could see ahead of me for a distance of about fifty meters; sitting at the top of a small grassy hill to our front appeared to be some barely visible, camouflaged bunkers that peeked out from the dirt about six inches above the surface. The black interior of the firing slits stood in contrast to the grass and sandy soil. I saw three of them, but it was hard to tell if there were more. I looked to my left and east of our position where a small, heavily treed hill was located on the fringe of the clearing about 125 meters away.

Six looked at me as I knelt behind the rocks with the other LTs, who had just joined us. "One Six, I want you to take your platoon and secure that small rise over there," Sonata said, pointing to our east. "We'll lay down covering fire from here on the bunkers, Mike. That position should afford you a better look at what we're facing. Move out in zero two minutes. Vinson, you and Bennett have your platoons lay down fire on the bunker line to cover their movement."

I began moving my platoon back from the rocks as the fire from 2nd and 3rd Platoons began to beat into the enemy's bunker line. The grass that covered the fringe of 352, and which led to the small hill, was about twenty inches high. It was the perfect height for us to low crawl through and would allow us to remain somewhat concealed. I warned everyone to stay down, because there was no cover other than the grass. I directed Gates' squad to lead in a staggered formation with 2nd, HQ, and 3rd Squads to follow. We hadn't gone twenty meters when automatic weapons' fire erupted to my front. An NVA machine gun soon added to the torrent.

Mac looked over at me. He was sprawled face down and was shouting into the radio handset at Six, "Six, we're getting slammed by AK and machine gun fire from our front and flank. Request more fire support."

The NVA guns continued to blaze away at us as we crawled forward. I heard men screaming at each other in front of me. I heard Van Artsdalen yell, "Clay's down!" I then saw him crawling back towards my position.

"Fuck, LT we've got machine gun fire up ahead that's six inches off the ground. Those mother fuckers killed Roosevelt. He was right in front of me and I saw his brains blown out. He was head shot through and through."

I looked at Van Artsdalen who was now crying, pounding the ground, and saying, "Shit" over and over again.

Gates then back-crawled into my location, almost kicking me in the head. "Sorry about that, LT, it's really weird up there. There's like a line where their machine gun and AK fire begins. It's grazing fire about twelve inches off the ground. If you're in back of the line there's no problem. If you're in front of it, it wastes you. That's what got Clay. I was watching. Milner and a new guy got clipped, too, when they tried to move up. There's no way we can get to Clay in that kill zone unless we can stop their fire."

I then heard rocket propelled grenades going off to our front, behind us and on the right flank near the rocks.

I yelled to my front, "Hodges, return the squads! Pull the squads back!"

Men were soon back-crawling to me as I directed them to return to the rocks and our previous location. Two men had wounds; Milner and a kid from 2nd Squad, Wacker. Milner had been shot in the arm and Wacker took a round in his leg. Neither looked life threatening. The automatic weapons' fire from the NVA was non-stop, as was the firing from the 2nd and 3rd Platoon.

I crawled backwards, turned around, and then ran bent over across to the clearing where we had come up the trail and dropped our rucks. Nelson, the platoon medic was busy bandaging and caring for Milner and Wacker. Sgt. Hodges was busy gathering Clay's ammo, water, and Cs from his ruck so they could be distributed amongst the platoon. I looked over at the rocks and saw Sonata and his radio operators crouched in a group. Six was looking at his map. I headed towards him.

As I reached the rocks, Sonata said to me, "I heard you lost a man and have two others wounded. 2nd lost one as well. There's plenty of pressure here and it looks like these dinks are interested in standing their ground. I want you to pull your platoon back down 100 meters from the clearing. 2nd and 3rd Platoons will pass through you. I just called for some air support and they're hustling jets towards us now. Let's get moving. I want to soften this area up and see if we can get some relief."

"I've got Clay still up there. We've got to get him, Six."

"Roger that, Mike. You'll get your chance soon."

After-Action Report: At 1545 hours, D/1-20 reports heavy contact receiving hand grenades, and automatic weapons' fire. Falling back to the fringe of the jungle at the hilltop, D/1-20 calls

for air support. At 1600 hours, Phantom F-4's raked the bunkers
of 352 with 20mm Gatling gun fire and napalm.

It was very close. The jets seemed to be just feet above our head when they were making their passes. I moved the men farther downhill when I saw napalm canisters tumbling over my head towards the bunker complex. The 20mm fire from the Phantoms was also unnerving. When those big Gatling guns would fire, it sounded like a groan from a huge, wounded animal. Then the rounds would impact with their explosive tips and all hell would break loose.

By the time the jets had finished their passes, the company had moved through my position and had formed a hasty defensive perimeter about 150 meters down from the clearing. My platoon had responsibility for the upper perimeter and we were grouped in three man positions. Sgt. Hodges had begun redistributing and checking ammo and water supplies with the squad leaders, as I had already passed the word for the platoon to eat and rearm in shifts. The medics were busy with the casualties near the company HQ.

Mac fired up some C4 and began some coffee as I dropped my ruck and took a long drink from my canteen.

"Take a good drink, LT. Here comes Six and he looks like he's fucking pissed."

I looked downhill at Sonata and his two radiomen who were trudging up to my position. When he arrived next to me, he dropped his rucksack, stretched his back, and then grabbed my canteen from my hand, took a long pull, and passed it back.

"Thanks, One Six. I'm out of water, the medics needed it."

"Ain't no big thang, Captain. Welcome to the luxury accommodations of 1st Platoon. We have water, ammo, fields of fire, and a solid perimeter," I said, as I pointed from left to right where our positions were located.

"I am happy to hear that, and you'll like this, Mike. 1-6 Infantry command wants us to probe Hill 352 again at 1800 hours. They want to see the effect of the jets and see just how determined these mother fuckers are. I want your platoon to lead until we get to the clearing. 2nd and 3rd will then pass through you to the rocks. Your platoon will then move up and join us on the left flank. We'll see if we can get to Clay."

Sixty-three minutes later, in torrential rain we reached the rocks with three platoons on line facing the bunkers. We had left our casualties at the tree line with Nelson and the 2nd Platoon medic, Kravitz.

We began our assault on Hill 352 and its bunker line with M79 grenades and M60 machine gun fire. The NVA did not hesitate to respond, returning fire with AKs, machine guns, and light mortar fire. To my left and uphill from our position where we had tried to advance before, machine gun fire now throbbed into our position, and I saw NVA moving from firing holes towards us. I ordered 2nd Squad and 1st Squad to direct their fire towards the hill and begin moving in that direction. I saw three NVA fall immediately.

To my right, 3rd Platoon was again catching hell. I could hear the thump of grenades and non-stop M16 and AK fire.

Mac yelled at me over the din of gunfire, "Six says he wants to break contact. We're not getting anywhere and 3rd Platoon is catching hell on the right flank. They've got four casualties. He wants us to move part way downhill and establish a defensive line so the rest of the company can fall back through us. We come down last."

I wasn't surprised. The NVA had clear fields of fire and had made it virtually impossible for us to advance. It also seemed to me that aircraft support was clearly not working, let alone our small arms' fire. Gates' squad could get no closer than fifteen meters to Clay's body.

Sgt. Hodges and I pulled the platoon down 100 meters from the clearing, put a squad out on each flank, and set a small skirmish line that the rest of the platoons could fall back through. I didn't have long to wait. The first soldiers of 2nd Platoon were soon passing through us and some of the troopers who were carrying wounded and dead looked a little shook up and anxious. Lt. Vinson, the 2nd's new platoon leader, seemed somewhat dazed as he passed by me. His uniform and helmet cover still had the brighter green sheen of an FNG to it, but now both carried smudges of mud. He had his eyes opened for sure.

"You okay?" I asked.

Vinson stopped and looked at me. He then nodded and said in low voice, "Yeah, I'm good." Then he turned and started down after his men. To me, he seemed a little disconnected.

"That LT has definitely had his first days in country filled with adventure," Mac said, as he had been standing next to me. "It's a great way to begin when you've got 350 days and a wake up to go."

I smiled and laughed under my breath at the irony, looked at him, and said, "Very true Mac. It's a rough way to start your first days in Vietnam, but we all have to start somewhere. Too bad for him it's here."

I didn't know at the time how prophetic that statement would become.

Chapter 28

IN AND OUT

Narrative: *Lt. McDonald-Low*

8 May 1968

After-Action Report: Remaining in heavy contact with a large unknown size NVA force, D/1-20 was forced to fall back with darkness into a poor night defensive position on the side of hill 352 vicinity BT072229. D/1-20 sustained 2 killed and 6 wounded. NVA casualties are estimated at 8 killed. D/1-20 established LP's and a night ambush. D/1-20 was unable to Dust Off any casualties because of the location and close contact with the enemy.

The night of 7 May and the early morning of 8 May were horrible. It had rained heavily and we were soaked. Everything I had was wet. We were spread out helter-skelter on the side of 352. It had been dusk by the time the company had passed through my platoon's position and set out to establish a secure perimeter. It wasn't by the book, as our perimeter roughly followed the terrain. I also deployed a two-man listening post and a three-man ambush patrol above us on the trail leading to the top of 352. The dead and wounded were with the company HQ and medics in the center of our perimeter.

Mac reported to me that Six had called battalion and reported that he had never seen an American infantry company get out-gunned before, and that there were more NVA in the bunkers than they suspected. I wasn't surprised.

I then walked over and corralled Lt. Charles Bennett, the new 3rd Platoon LT. A graduate of ranger school, he had been in country three weeks. Dark-haired, 23-years-old, squarely built, educated and from the East Coast, Bennett was low key and didn't have a whole lot to say. He was still too new to compare what had happened today to anything else in his short infantry life. As the rain beat down upon us, we sat side by side under a poncho and used C4 to heat some coffee. For the next twenty minutes we shared stories of home before heading back to our individual platoon HQs.

All night long it rained, the wounded screamed, yelled, and talked, their morphine injections giving them hallucinations and vivid nightmares. It was downright creepy and a little disheartening. Nobody relaxed, as we were fearful the screams and shouts were giving away our location and that we would soon be attacked. The radios squawked all night.

Luckily, the night passed without any further contact from the enemy. We now faced the tough job of getting our dead and wounded out and fresh ammo and water in. I recalled the LP and ambush patrol, and the company moved back down Hill 352 to the valley floor. We headed slowly to a location near our previous night defensive position of 6 May. At 0940 hours, we finished establishing a perimeter near the paddy, across from the ville', and waited for the Dust Off chopper that was inbound.

Once we heard, and then saw the chopper, Sgt. Gates ran into the paddy and set a yellow smoke grenade on the paddy wall. He then started guiding the bird in. Both his hands and arms were raised straight up in the air. The smoke streamed in front of him. As the slick slowed and came in on its final approach, AK fire started in on the chopper from above the ville'. I saw the bird shake from a hit, and then it flared up and out, rolling east looking for altitude. Gates ran and sloshed back to us.

I looked over at Six, who was standing with the headquarters radiomen, medics, and the casualties. There were twelve men acting as litter bearers, huddled around the wounded and dead.

"Is that Lt. Bennett on the right flank? Mike, tell him to get some squads on the other side of the paddy so we can get a bird in here. Use your radio, I'm busy with resupply and battalion."

I looked back at Sonata, nodded and turned to Mac.

Macintyre was already on it, calling Bennett and 2nd Platoon telling them to move back to the ville' and secure it.

"Six, it's going to take a good forty minutes for Two Six to get that area cleared. Let's bring water and ammo in first. I'm just about out of 7.62 for the M60s and most men have only two or three magazines of M16 ammo. Some of my guys haven't had water since yesterday afternoon. We're rationing, but it won't last long. We can have them drop water and ammo into our position on the fly. No stopping. We'll pop smoke, and they can drop the good stuff right on us."

At 1234 hours, the brave crew of a Minuteman slick resupplied us under intense fire when water and ammo kicked out of the chopper and landed on our position. The slick had barely slowed down, passing just fifty feet off the deck, when he made the drop. 2nd Platoon, positioned around and above the ville' had no effect in slowing the NVA rounds fired at the chopper.

Now we had to get our casualties out.

The Dust Off came roaring in with two Firebird gunship escorts who immediately began pounding the hill above the ville' with rockets and mini-gun fire. I watched the Dust Off flare into our LZ and land. Our company's new head medic jumped off the chopper as the two Dust Off crewmen threw out three, large wooden boxes.

I then heard two shots ring out and watched the medic fall to the ground. He immediately sat up, stood, and limped back to the chopper holding his side, which now had a red stain spreading on his fatigue jacket. He reached into the chopper, grabbed his medic supply bag and threw it down on the ground. Then he crawled into the bird, sat, and started waving for the casualties. The IV drips were already dangling inside the Dust Off.

Four men carried a soldier wrapped in a poncho, his booted feet hanging incongruously out of the end. Four other men carried another dead GI, while others helped the medics with the six wounded. The wounded men looked as if they would recover although the strained faces of each man painted a grimmer picture. None of the men carried their weapons or rucks, as they had already been stripped, and their gear and ammo passed out among their squad. Most M79 grenadiers now also carried M16s from the casualties.

The crewmen of the Dust Off helped to quickly load the wounded and dead. Smoke from the grenade was still thick and whirled around the chopper from its swirling blades. As the Dust Off crew chief loaded the last casualty, the chopper began to lift off, nose heavy. It seemed to take forever to gain altitude, and it appeared to be just inches above the rice paddy floor.

I continued to watch the chopper as it cleared the valley and began its rise to higher, safer altitudes. The two gunships had also departed with the Dust Off when another burst of automatic weapons' fire from above the ville' slammed into 2nd Platoon. I then heard Six get the call from Bennett. He had a man down, leg wound, and he needed a Dust Off.

We completed another Dust Off at 1255 hours without incident at the landing zone.

The wooden boxes left for us from the first Dust Off contained thirty-six LAWs; a small, tubular shaped, shoulder fired anti-tank weapon that had no recoil. When the LAW fires, flames shoot out the back as the explosive projectile rockets out the front. We usually didn't have them, but Sonata thought they just might help, so he had requested their delivery. I liked the idea.

Later that afternoon, 2nd and 3rd Platoons reconnoitered the ville' and the nearby brush of the paddy. My platoon provided security for the HQ and pretty much was taking a breather. My men had spent the afternoon changing their socks, eating, smoking, and napping in shifts. I watched Doc Nelson check each trooper for ailments. I thought about the casualties we had taken and how indispensable our medics were to us. They were the first person called when there was real trouble, or just a minor problem.

UNACCOUNTED

At 1750 hours, the company moved back to our previous night defensive position at BT067238. It felt just like home.

After-Action Report: Nearby, two more 198th LIB companies were brought into the operation. D/1-6 was moved out of the Burlington Trail AO and was transported from the vicinity of LZ East to LZ West at BT990250 in one lift. By 0930 hours, C/1-6 was moved from LZ West into the area southwest of LZ Center at BT024224. New to the fray, units of 1/20 Infantry, A/1-20 and B/1-20 were moved from LZ Ross and inserted into the area just west of C/1-6 at BT019269.

There were now twice as many American infantry companies in the area near LZ Center, under the operational control of the command of the HQ/1-6 infantry, than there had been a day before. The additional troops, however, did not deter the NVA forces. At BT080855, two 122-mm rockets impacted 20 meters in front of bunker #20 on LZ Center. The suspected launch site was at BT080263. The NVA had announced their intention to stay and fight.

At 1229 hours, B/1-6 was in contact with NVA forces at BT056246 with one WHA. They had automatic weapons' fire only 50 meters to their front. The Dust Off was completed, however, by 1255 hours. When the NVA opened up with a .51 caliber machine gun from BT056226, the unit requested an air strike.

By 1400 hours, B/1-6 had made contact with an unknown size NVA force in a bunker complex to their front. They killed 13 NVA who were dug in at several positions, and captured two AK-47's and, significantly, one Soviet DshKM 12.7mm Anti-Aircraft machine gun. The NVA used these heavy machine guns to cover landing zones. This particular AA gun was equipped with a large circular anti-aircraft sight and shoulder braces for the operator who crouched in the hole to the left of the gun to get elevation for the shooting at aircraft. One soldier from B/1-6 moved into position with a light anti-tank (LAW) weapon, and knocked out the enemy crew of the weapon. Other soldiers in the unit successfully assaulted three or four enemy positions adjacent to the AA gun. By 1516 hours, the soldiers of B/1-6 had called in Dust Off for 7 wounded and one heat casualty.

At 1640 hours, B/1-6 received enemy mortar fire at BT057227, resulting in an additional wounded. By 1715 hours, their interpreter was killed, and two additional soldiers were wounded and dusted off at 1740 hours. At 1830 hours, B/1-6 was being mortared, and at 1925 hours, they engaged an NVA force at BT057211 killing 3 NVA.

C/1-6, who had been moving eastward from their LZ at BT024224, reached the hilltop at BT048226, killing 1 NVA and capturing 1 AK-47, and three Chi-Com grenades. By 1940 hours, B/1-6 killed another NVA at BT048226. Additional NVA were then observed on the ridgeline at BT057230. Because the NVA were operating boldly and at full strength, B/1-6 and C/1-6 moved into a night defensive position together at BT057227 in the vicinity of the Nui Hoac Ridge.

Chapter 29

TOO CLOSE

Narrative: *Lt. McDonald–Low*

9 May 1968

After-Action Report: In the early morning of 9 May at 0445 hours, B/1-6 received 20 rounds of 60-mm mortar fire. In addition, one RPG round went over their perimeter from the NNE. Gunships on station at 0509 hours received small arms' fire as they attacked. After the gunships returned from re-arming, they had two secondary explosions on the targets. They also took .51 caliber fire from BT042217. At 0700 hours, B/1-6 was still taking enemy rocket fire. At 0955 hours, they were taking mortar fire from SW of their location and by 1105 hours, they had received 14 more mortar rounds.

Later on 9 May, B/1-6 and C/1-6 moved eastward along the ridge towards BT057228 with C/1-6 taking the lead. At 1100 hours, D/1-20, assaulted a hill further east on the ridge at BT062229. Helix 25 had spotted at least 30 NVA dug in a bunker position on the hill. At 1150 hours, while moving eastward toward that same enemy location from up on the ridgeline, C/1-6 received heavy weapons fire from BT060228. Because of the volume of fire, B/1-6 and C/1-6 consolidated their position at BT057227, and decided to wait for an air strike. They had 16 wounded and 5 heat casualties when assaulting the hill.

At LZ Center, the enemy continued their mortar and rocket attacks throughout the entire day. 7 men were wounded and dusted off after the attacks.

At 1045 hours, we moved to the top of Hill 352. We started coming under AK fire as soon as we reached the clearing. I moved my platoon down the fringe of the clearing to the left, while 2nd Platoon moved to occupy the rocky out cropping. 3rd Platoon joined them as they arrived. Sonata and the HQ moved with the 2nd.

As soon as I started maneuvering the platoon back to where we lost Clay, we came under viscous fire. They had waited just long enough for us to separate ourselves from the company. We were now momentarily cut off. I looked over my right shoulder and saw men from 2nd Platoon running to the rocks under sporadic AK gunfire.

I called Six and told him of our predicament, and he told me that they were going to break out the LAWs and to put our heads down. It worked. As the explosions from the LAWs went off, I pulled my platoon back off the flank and joined the others at the west end of the rocks. As Van Artsdalen came past me he said, "Those fuckin' dinks moved

Clay. I got to his helmet, but his body was gone." I nodded, and then high crawled over to Sonata.

"They moved Clay, Six. They've also got the same fields of fire burning us."

"Roger that. Let's lay down some serious fire on those dinks and use up our LAWs," Sonata said to me, and then Bennett who had joined us behind the rocks.

I high crawled and ran back to my platoon.

The LAWs started going off almost immediately. I looked to my left and saw three go off almost simultaneously from my 2nd and 3rd Squads, as Cerutti continued nonstop on the 60. Others were shooting their 16s. Van Artsdalen and Zapata fired two more LAWs. I felt the heat and heard the "whoosh" from the back blasts as they did.

From all the LAWs that were expended, I saw two, small secondary explosions that made contact with the NVA bunkers. It was hard to tell whether our barrage was working because there was little return fire from the NVA. As our rate of fire diminished and the LAWs ended; machine gun and AK fire again erupted from the bunker line. The ferocity of the fire included several RPG rounds that pounded the rocks we were using for cover. I ran and high crawled back over to Six and he was pissed.

"Shit. We just lost Lieutenant Vinson. He was backing his men off the rocks, covering them, and he was hit by an RPG blast. Shrapnel hit him in the head. Gates, your squad leader saw it, ran over, and pulled him back. Gates was then shot in the hand and elbow. Another guy got clipped as well. Still checking that ID. We got Vinson, but part of his head was blown off and there's no way we could do anything for him."

I looked over at the rolled poncho on the ground, and I recognized where Vinson was now covered. The medics were treating Sgt. Gates and three other men.

Six told me to move back to the edge of the clearing and let the wounded, medics, and then everyone pass through my platoon as before. "We better do it quick because I've got some Phantoms rolling on the bunkers to cover our movement in zero five minutes."

Cpt. Sonata had reported to HQ that we were unable to get closer than 50 meters of the NVA perimeter. The AK and machine gun fire from the NVA was now so intense he had requested an air strike on the hilltop to cover our disengagement.

As the last elements of the company and 3rd Platoon passed by me heading downhill, I saw movement to the east of the bunker line beyond the rocks. Van Artsdalen, Lockhart, and Zapata, who were still holding position at the edge of the clearing, saw it too and immediately started laying down fire with their 16s and M79. I saw two NVA immediately drop and a third running, but then blown skyward by a 79 round.

I yelled at the closest man I could see, "Lockhart, get 1st Squad back here, we're leaving and the jets are coming!"

I could see the F-4s just circling to the east of us. Helix 25 was a white spot overhead.

I knew B/1-6 and C/1-6 were several hundred meters to our west waiting for Helix 25 to hit BT075225 with 250-pound bombs. That's why we were on the move, too. The concussion from a 250 pounder is not something anyone wanted to be near. If the blast and shrapnel didn't kill you, the concussion would if you were too close.

Mac, listening on the radio handset, then yelled at me, "We gotta go LT, the jets are cleared and rolling."

Lockhart, Van Artsdalen, and the remainder of 1st Squad reached me and we all turned and started scrambling downhill after the company. Automatic weapons' fire was now directed not only at us, but also at the overhead Phantoms.

A giant boom behind our location made us all hit the ground. There was another crushing explosion followed by another. The concussions washed over us. The ground shook.

20mm cannon fire groaned from the F4s as they worked the ridge top. It was the only sound I heard as the NVA had stopped returning fire. I quickly got to my feet and yelled at everyone to start moving. Lockhart and Zapata had just ran past me when I looked back up the trail and saw a canister of napalm. It was tumbling fifty feet in the air end over end towards the hilltop above. Sunlight glinted off the bright aluminum of its tube shaped canister. It landed short and exploded on the clearing where we had dropped our rucks. I then heard a secondary explosion from another bomb and pieces of errant shrapnel tore downhill above our heads. As I looked toward the sound, a small piece of something hit and slashed the left side of my forehead, knocking me ass over teakettle. I landed on my back, wondering what the hell had happened.

Nelson rushed up to me and started shaking me and said, "LT, you just got real lucky. Couple stitches and you'll be fine."

I sat up and, in a fog, watched as Nelson applied a field dressing to my head. Mac grabbed my helmet and stood next to me watching Nelson. After Nelson tied the knot so the bandage would stay in place they both helped me to my feet. Mac passed me my 16, keeping the helmet.

Neither said a word. The remainder of the squad had stopped behind us, waiting.

I didn't feel so fine; I was dazed but I said, "Okay, I'm good. Let's go."

My movement down the hill was surreal. I thought of nothing but my feet moving, my heart pounding, and my labored breathing. I kept having to rub my right eye as the blood seeped from the bandage, which was now soaked with blood. It seemed like hours for us to reach our previously occupied perimeter of 7 May, but in real time it was about fifteen minutes.

When we finally arrived, the company quickly settled into digging out our now familiar fighting pits. During the time it took for Sgt. Hodges to verify our portion of the perimeter and to check firing positions, Nelson had taped four, big butterfly stitches onto my forehead. He had worked quickly after cleaning the gash, applying each piece of tape as quickly and painlessly as he could. It hurt like hell and made tears run down my face with the blood. After the final taped stitch was in place, he patted the wound dry and stood back admiring his work.

"Looks like a dueling scar, LT. Very distinguished."

"Thanks, Nelson. It's just what I've always wanted."

"Here's some aspirin LT, it'll help if it hurts. It looks good enough to keep you going. I'm going to put a bandage over it to help keep it clean."

"Thanks for the help and the opinion, Nelson. I need to get back to work." I sounded a lot tougher than I felt.

The wounded, plus Vinson, were moved and positioned with the medics just below Sonata and the HQ group. Six had received orders that we were to spend the night where we were, and to block any NVA forces attempting to flee south towards us. There would be no Dust Off.

After hearing the news Sonata asked me, "Mike, if you're up to it, can you remove the personal effects of Lt. Vinson? I have casualty reports and battalion to deal with."

It wasn't the best job I'd ever been given, but it was one that had to be done. I told him, "Roger, I can do that, Six."

I walked down through the drizzle to where I found Nelson, still administering to the wounded. The two new platoon medics, whom I didn't really know, were helping him. Sgt. Gates was incoherent, babbling away, already high on morphine. When he saw me he yelled out at the top of his lungs, "LT! Son of a bitch, I fucked up. Shoulda' zigged when I zagged. I got that new LT back though. He was fuckin' dead."

He then started talking about the surf back home and how he was going to "stomp it" after graduating college and marrying the love of his life, Vicky Bonner. Morphine took you places.

As Gates continued his one-sided conversation with me, I turned and could see Vinson's body rolled up in a poncho. His helmet sat on his covered chest.

I knelt down next to the poncho and removed the helmet. I opened the poncho and took a quick glance at Vinson's mangled face and head. It was gruesome and horrible; his left eye was missing, as was much of the left side of his face and head. I looked away. I turned my attention to his arms, which were folded across his chest. I removed his wedding ring. It slid right off his finger, which luckily was extended in rigor. I checked his pockets and found a letter and some Vietnamese money. There was nothing else. I covered him back up. I then checked his ruck and found Cs, underwear, socks, and towels. His toothbrush was in a plastic tube. It all looked brand new, which it was.

I carried the remaining effects of Lt. Vinson back to Sonata and deposited them in his hand, wordlessly, and walked back to my platoon.

I reinforced my position at the trailhead above and set an ambush another 50 meters up. As the late afternoon turned to evening, a sense of uncertainty and jumpiness set in on the company. The first Claymore went off just as it turned dusk and shortly afterwards another position briefly opened up with their M16. There was no return fire. I immediately told Six I was pulling my ambush patrol, as I was fearful they would get their asses shot off by our own men. I hated moving men this close to dark, remembering Robbin, but I yelled for them the whole way up so that they knew I was coming. As the last bit of light faded, I successfully returned all five men back to the perimeter.

It remained quiet until about 0300 hours when nervous, anxious riflemen opened up on unknown sounds and one of the wounded started yelling and screaming, and soon they all were. It was disturbing, but somehow appropriate given where we were.

My head was pounding. The night wore on.

Chapter 30

THROUGH THE CANOPY

Narrative: *Spec. 4 Clifford Van Artsdalen*

10 May 1968

The morning of 10 May dawned clear. It was going to be hot and humid. My squad and I were exhausted from being on the side of Hill 352. I missed Clay terribly, and the other men who were killed and wounded only made me more angry and sad. Zapata, Cerutti, Lockhart, and I were the last of the "originals" from Hawaii in my squad. We all wondered where the dinks had moved Roosevelt, and why.

I had also grown tired of having our casualties wait overnight for Dust Off. It seemed cruel to me, but the truth was that we didn't have much of a choice.

Zapata said it best when we were having our morning C-4 and coffee, "This place is a fuckin shit hole. We kill them and they seem to have even more backing their play. We bomb the shit out of 'em and they come up for more. It really ain't no big thang, if you know what I mean. I've been on that fuckin' hill laying down fire for five days, and I tell ya home boys; I want those bunkers. I know we can take 'em, but Six calls us back. Sure, we gonna die, but I am tired of fuckin' around."

"We're all tired of this too, Zapata," said Lt. McDonald-Low who had just walked up behind Zapata, who was sitting on the edge of his fighting pit.

The LT had his helmet off, and his head bandage was stained with blood. I looked away, trying not to stare.

"Sorry LT. I was just sayin' we should get it on and kick their ass."

"We all want to Zapata. It isn't up to us what we do; it depends on what we're facing as a company and how many men we're prepared to lose to take those bunkers. Six and I both agree we need to overcome their firepower first. The bombs and napalm aren't working. The truth is we're hurting them, but we're bleeding away up here. Every time we assault that hill we take casualties. The Big Six at 1-6 Infantry has the picture; we've got new orders."

"Sergeant Hodges, Van Artsdalen, we've got about sixty minutes to get moving. The company is heading back to the paddy at the ville' and setting a hasty perimeter. We've got a Dust Off coming in followed by ammo and water. We'll recon slowly on the way down."

"Roger that, LT," I said to Lt. McDonald-Low's back. He was already heading to where Hodges was now talking to the other squad leaders.

Our platoon led the way down that morning to the ville'. We were in front as usual and I had point, which is where I wanted to be. Zapata and Cerutti were staggered each about fifteen feet behind me with the rest of the platoon following them.

I didn't see or hear anything all morning. When I reached the ville' it was empty. I stopped the squad and called for the LT to come forward. I was already dripping wet from the heat and the load on my back.

One Six came forward with Sgt. Hodges and Macintyre. I could see he had ditched his steel pot. "Sergeant Hodges. Have the squads set the perimeter on this side. Dust Off is in zero five minutes. Van Artsdalen you've got the smoke."

When I dropped the yellow smoke grenade on the paddy wall I expected trouble, but nothing happened. The bird saw the smoke, and I guided it in. Still nothing. Vinson, Sgt. Gates and the other dead and wounded were loaded aboard the Dust Off. Nothing. I wondered if the NVA were on a chow break, because the whole thing went down without a shot. I wasn't surprised to see that the LT didn't go. His head wound didn't appear that serious, and he acted more pissed about it than anything else.

Resupply of ammo and water hurtled into our position through the canopy at 1410 hours.

I watched the water bags as they rolled out of each side of the slick. They tumbled in mid-air from the speed of the chopper and then nose-dived through the brush. Two water bags landed right next to 2nd Platoon and another landed about fifty meters in front of us. I was thankful they didn't hit anyone, because the impact of an eighty-pound bag of water would have been horrible. Zapata and Cerutti hustled to the front and drug them back. The ammo crates were a different story.

The sound of the wooden ammo crates crashing into our position at fifty plus miles per hour had GIs running for cover everywhere. It was similar to mortar rounds, without the explosion or shrapnel. Each crate contained three metal boxes of ammunition. Most of it was .556 for the M16s, and the bigger, heavier boxes were the 7.62 for the M60s. In total, they dropped sixteen crates. Ten were for the M16s, two for the M79s and four were for the 60s. Nobody was hit, though there were several near misses. One crate of .556 ammo was not recovered, location unknown.

Having fresh water and ammo made everyone feel as if it were Christmas. It was a feeling that didn't last long. We had also received marching orders that would finally take us off 352. We were being routed back to where we had established our night perimeter at BT083247, the location of our first night in the valley with Bravo Company. Our orders directed us to evacuate the vicinity and make foot movement to LZ Center at first light the following morning. They wanted us to stand-down, refit, and re-man. They originally had us scheduled to go to LZ Ross, but apparently thought the long hike for our now half-sized infantry company would be too treacherous.

The news of us leaving Hill 352 and the valley and heading for stand-down at LZ Center was greeted with somber elation. The good news was that we were leaving. The bad news was that we all felt we had unfinished business on 352; Roosevelt's body was still there. We also were not flying out, and it would be a long hump through bad country to get to LZ Center. I knew the NVA would not let us leave quietly.

After-Action Report: On 10 May 1968, the mortar attacks also continued against the units in the field. At 1010 hours, B/1-6 was hit by two rounds from BT051223. At 1140 hours, Helix 25 called in air strikes at BT051225, BT055227, BT062227 and BT065227. Two secondary explosions were observed at BT058227. In spite of the air strikes, at 1245 hours, B/1-6 and C/1-6 received intense mortar fire resulting in 1 KHA and 2 WHA of B/1-6, while C/1-6 had 1 WHA and 1 heat casualty in shock. By 1346 hours, they had dusted off 9 WHA, 1 KHA, and 1 heat casualty. Later that day, the USAF "Spooky" C130 gunship arrived to provide support. Ground fire was observed by C/1-6 and B/1-6 coming from BT044224, and BT082237.

When the air strikes began in the late morning of 10 May, A/1-6 and E/1-6 used the occasion to begin moving. They were hit with enemy mortar fire with negative results. By 1517 hours, A/1-6 observed two VC in the open carrying a mortar tube at BT057224. At 2228 hours, C/1-20, a unit under the operational control of the 1-6 Infantry, occupied the position at BT057288. They received intense weapons' fire and small arms' fire from 300 meters to their southwest. Their forward observer was wounded. Moments later, they reported enemy movement on all sides. When the Dust Off arrived to extract the wounded, they took ground fire from the west. Gunships supported the extraction, and negative contact was experienced after 2325 hours.

In spite of all the firepower that had been directed in the vicinity of LZ Center, the enemy continued their mortar attacks on the firebase on 10 May. LZ Center was hit at 0758 hours, and again at 0825 hours. At 1130 hours, the Americal Division Commander, Major General Koster, arrived at LZ Baldy for a briefing on the situation around LZ Center.

Chapter 31

Narrative: *Spec. 4 Clifford Van Artsdalen*
11 May 1968

After-Action Report: At 0645 hours, Delta 1-20 departed their NDP location BT083247, heading north and across the valley through a small village. D/1-20 headed up out of the valley at BT076250 following an old streambed and trail. D/1-20 followed the streambed north as it meandered to where it reached the top of the ridgeline at BT070258 at a "Y" trail intersection.

I remembered this day clearly. How could I forget?

After crossing through the paddies from our NDP, I arrived at a small opening in the bush near the base of two adjoining hills. I stepped into the opening through some big banana leafed plants and bamboo. As I looked at the trail, the morning sun made it seem golden in the early morning light. A dry, stony creek bed seemed to follow the trail as it wound its way up the hill. After stopping to listen and carefully look at the surroundings, I began my trudge up the trail.

UNACCOUNTED

I took my time. The LT had told me he hated following a trail, especially here, but he had his orders. The bush went from thick and canopied, to low scrub and trees with openings and small grassy patches. I was thinking the little patches were perfect for cattle, though I hadn't seen any. The area was deserted. The few hooches I passed to get to the opening in the bush had been empty. It was a ghost town.

It took me about fifty minutes to carefully work my way to the top of the hill and reach a "Y" in the trail. It had been stop and go for me on the way up, mainly because I didn't want to get my ass shot off. When I reached the "Y" I crouched down and gave the hand signal for everyone to stop. I listened and watched. The main trail continued to my left, while a smaller trail led downhill to my front. I was at the junction. It was where the LT had told me to stop.

I listened and I looked. Nothing. No sound. I didn't like it. It was just too quiet and empty. I was thinking the movement here had seemed a little too easy and the dinks didn't let anyone off the hook easily in the Que Son. I looked back down trail and watched the LT coming towards me, dragging Macintyre behind him, the coiled loop of the cord that ran to the radio between them. He looked stressed. His jungle shirt was stained from sweat, and I could see a darker area on his right shoulder and chest from where he had bled after being hit in the head by shrapnel. He was talking on the headset. His helmet was strapped to his ruck. Everyone else was at the ready and watching the bush.

"Roger that, Six," I heard the LT say. He then looked at me as he passed the handset back to Macintyre and said, "Van, split your squad. I want you and two men to go up trail towards LZ Center, about seventy meters. Recon and secure. The other three I want down that trail about fifty meters, same thing. I'll bring 2nd Squad up to secure this location. Let's move."

I looked at Lockhart and Zapata. They had already heard the LT and had started to move. I then looked at my remaining squad members, "Jackson, take the two new guys and go down trail fifty meters and secure that end. Cerutti, move down trail ten meters and cover this area with the 60. I'll be up trail with Lockhart and Zapata. Keep your eyes open."

I turned and followed my best friends and, when I looked back, I could see the LT had his map case out and Captain Sonata had just joined him with his RTO. "Meeting of the minds," I thought and wondered what was next.

I then heard Zapata curse as he swiped at a leech on his pant leg, "Fucking leeches, they always like it when it's quiet."

I looked ahead and saw that the trail widened to an open, brightly lit grassy area, and beyond it I could see the top slope of 348, but not LZ Center. To the right of the clearing was a rocky hillside that ran up and away. It was part of the ridge that ran down as a finger from 348 and it was covered with clumps of brush and big rocks the further up the hill it went. Immediately to our left and bordering the trail and grassy opening was a steep hill covered in trees and jungle growth. "Not a problem, there," I thought, it was just too fucking thick.

I looked ahead and saw that Lockhart had just reached the spot where the vegetation on either side of the trail ended and an open grassy area began. He stopped and crouched, signaling us to stop. "Good move," I thought. After about fifteen seconds he turned and looked back at us. His hand pointed forward, and he began to move again. Zapata and I followed.

Zapata reached the grassy opening and started forward. Ten seconds later I saw two ChiCom stick grenades floating through the air towards Zapata and Lockhart. Before I could yell, a machine gun raked their position, hitting them both. I watched them recoil, their bodies dancing and contorting from the impacts. Before I could move, the grenades went off and threw shrapnel, luckily missing me. I turned to where the machine gun fire had come from, raised my M79 and shot an HE round towards the position. I ejected the cartridge and reloaded.

The first AK round hit me in the leg and it knocked me down on my ass. My first thought was that something had bitten me. As I sat there, I looked down and saw my fatigue pant torn with blood seeping from a hole in my thigh, turning the green pant reddish. It was weird how white my leg was. As I contemplated the sheer madness of what I was witnessing, two more rounds hit me in the chest and hip. As I fell backwards, I remembered wondering what had happened. That was my last thought as my life eased out of me and I faded into blackness.

After-Action Report: At 0840 hours 1st Platoon elements of D/1-20 came under heavy machine gun, grenade and RPG fire up-trail vicinity BT068255.

At the "Y" 1st Platoon had just sent three soldiers further up trail towards LZ Center to secure the trail positions. Three soldiers were also sent north down trail for security. As company command elements of D/1-20 reached the "Y" a machine gun with grazing fields of fire raked downhill from the ridge that led from the direction of LZ Center. Other NVA soldiers were observed firing from the head of the "Y" in concealed positions.

1-6 Infantry reports D/1-20 is pinned down and receiving intense automatic weapons' fire, small arms' fire and grenades. Lead elements of D/1-20 were cut off from the main body. Adding to the difficulty was the dense wooded terrain and the fact that D/1-20 elements were spread out over 1/8 mile down the trail from the main ambush. The only access was up the small streambed that the lead elements had followed. No passage without machete and strenuous cutting could be made away from the streambed.

Lead elements of D/1-20, not initially KHA or WHA returned fire toward suspected NVA positions. Chi-com grenades exploded near the "Y". Mid and rear elements of D/1-20 surged slowly forward and joined the firefight maneuvering to get D/1-20 WHA and KHA out of harms way. One by one D/1-20 soldiers began to form up and secure the upper ridgeline and trailhead.

At 0920 hours, D/1-20 is able to call for Dust Off of WHA and KHA after cutting out a LZ on the side of the ridge. Under sporadic automatic weapons' fire, a Dust Off helicopter was able to come in and hover in-position on the small cut out side on the side of the ridge. D/1-20 overloaded it with 10 KHA's and WHA's. Protected by gunships overhead, the Dust Off made its lift out of the LZ, but sustained brief machine gun fire and took a .51 cal hit to its tail. The impact failed to bring down the helicopter and it wobbled on to LZ Baldy with all casualties.

At 1015 hours, a 1-6 Infantry resupply slick reports it received 15 to 20 automatic weapons' fire and took one hit in blade, and was going to Chu Lai for repair. At 1020 hours, D/1-20 was able to finally break contact and is given orders to move down into the valley and re-route to LZ Center. After a long march to the west to BT044248, surviving elements of D/1-20 are able to make their way back up the west ridge and into LZ Center. D/1-20 reports that it was unable to recover 3 KHA.

At 1148 hours, A/1-6 has made contact at BT065254, has two WHA at BT067253, and is receiving heavy automatic weapons' and small arms' fire. They had just entered a draw and spotted D/1-20 soldiers killed in an ambush previously, when the enemy engaged them. A/1-6 in its initial assault was able to recover 2 of the 3 KHA's of D/1-20. At 1320 hours, the final lift for D/1-20 leaving LZ Center was completed and they are sent to LZ Ross for reserve. D/1-20 reported 11 May casualties KHA 5, WHA 7 and one soldier KHA/MIA.

Chapter 32

THE PRICE OF VICTORY

12 –18 May 1968

Between 12 May and 18 May, it would take the combined forces of companies A/1-20, B/1-20, C/1-20, A/1-6, D/1-6 and the Recon Platoon from E/1-6 to eventually reach and take the high ground and bunker complexes of Nui Hoac Ridge and Hill 352. A/1-20 recovered the remains of Specialist 4 Roosevelt Clay on 21 May. Specialist 4 Van Artsdalen was reported MIA, and assumed to be KIA.

After-Action Report: The enemy bunker complex on the east side of Hill 352 was later deemed impregnable once the positions were examined after being abandoned by the NVA. It was discovered that a company sized force of NVA regulars were positioned in well fortified, dug-in bunkers over six feet deep with reinforced covers, and S-shaped tunnels for entrance or exit. The enemy was armed with small arms, automatic weapons, heavy machine guns, RPG's, and 60-mm mortars. These positions were found well supplied with ammunition, food, and water. The enemy had excellent fields of fire on any attacking force, as the gently sloping ridges around Hill 352 had few normal terrain features to provide cover, and little foliage due to air strikes in the area. The day of the attacks by D/1-20 and B/1-6 were bright, sunny and extremely hot. Helix 25 reported the bunker complex, "Looks like an old U.S. firebase."

A Medal of Honor (SFC Finnis D. McCleery, A Company, 1st Battalion, 6th Infantry), and many other distinguished awards for valor were earned and eventually awarded to men of those units participating in the battle for Nui Hoac Ridge, Hill 352.

Intense fighting with the 2nd NVA Division continued in the area of Nui Hoac Ridge until 26 May. Numerous other small conflicts continued in the area until late July.

Cumulative Losses
Operation Wheeler/Wallowa
5 May 1968 – 31 July 1968
U.S. Forces: 122 Killed, 715 Wounded, 1 MIA
NVA Forces: 865 Killed, 560 Wounded (estimated)

PART TWO

FINDING 1165

Duty is what one expects of others.

Oscar Wilde

Chapter 33

HURRY UP AND WAIT

M. McDonald-Low

2011

EMAIL

Carne, Ray Civ JPAC J2 to Michael McDonald-Low

10 Feb 2011

Sorry, Michael, it's been very busy at the office.

As of last week planning meeting, the mission is still a go. There is a money issue right now for the whole mission, has something to do with the Fiscal Year budgeting. The cutoff date is 10 March, meaning if there is no funding available for Vietnam mission by then, the mission will be a cancel. Until then we have to keep the ball rolling as if we have the money already.

This case is weather driven, so it could be next year. I am hoping for the best; seems like every year we go through this. I will keep you posted on any news.

I will let you know weekly or if any new development comes up.

Let me know if you need anything from me. I'm usually available.

Ray

———

EMAIL
Carne, Ray Civ JPAC J2 to Michael McDonald-Low
31 Mar 2011

Good morning Michael,

The mission for the JFA in August is a go as a whole, but your investigation team is not going. We were cancelled for the 11–3VM mission and now it is leaning toward 11–4VM being cancelled, too. The goal for 11–4VM was to send a small 4–man team instead of the normal 15, and would only do interviews without a survey.

I am working on getting us a new mission date.

Ray

———

EMAIL
Carne, Ray Civ JPAC J2 to Michael McDonald-Low
25 Jul 2011

Dear Michael,

The time has come for us to start planning your mission, again. What would be a better time for you to accompany the team to

Vietnam? FY12-2VM is 7 Mar; you will accompany the team for the first week. If you want a later date, FY12-3 is 20 May.

Ray

———

EMAIL

Michael McDonald-Low to Carne, Ray Civ JPAC J2

26 July 2011

Ray,

I'll take March 7. Sooner the better!

Michael

———

EMAIL

Carne, Ray Civ JPAC J2 to Michael McDonald-Low

6 Jan 2012

Michael,

Just got word from my boss. It's official. Your "Orders" are attached and you are good to go for March 7, 2012!

Ray

Chapter 34

MISSION LINE-UP

M. McDonald-Low

2012

EMAIL

McLaren, Favian CW2 JPAC J2 to Michael McDonald-Low

1 Feb 2012

Mr. McDonald-Low,

I want to personally welcome you to our JPAC Investigation Team for Joint Field Activity (JFA) 106. I've been anxious to meet with you and begin this very important investigation. As it turns out, I will be departing the Friday before your arrival on island as part of the Joint Advance Work (JAW) along with my linguists. I'll meet up with you once you arrive to Vietnam on 7 March with the main body personnel.

Again, I look forward to meeting and working with you soon. If you have any concerns or need anything, just let me know. I have one of my best analysts leading this investigation, Sgt. Wesley Martin (USMC). SSG Jessica Hernandez will be our team NCOIC for this mission and is assigned to accompany you once you arrive to Hawaii.

Very Respectfully,

Favian J. McLaren, Chief Warrant Officer 2, Military Intelligence

———

EMAIL

Hernandez, Jessica SSG JPAC J2 to Michael McDonald-Low

23 Feb 2012

Michael,

Welcome to the team! We will be conducting your case brief the morning of February 29th. Since you want to see all the sites, your JPAC Tour will be following your case brief, at 1030. You will enjoy it. It should last about 45 minutes. You are scheduled to meet with Commanding General, Major General Thomas on 1 March from 1330-1400. I will show you where this is.

See you soon!

SSG Jessica Hernandez, USA

Joint POW/MIA Accounting Command

———

EMAIL

Carne, Ray Civ JPAC J2 to Michael McDonald-Low

23 Feb 2012

Michael,

Just to give you the overview of the whole IT1 mission and how important it is to have you to assist us with Case 1165, I am attaching the entire mission overview, below.

Ray

———

From: McLaren, Favian CW2 JPAC J2
23 Feb 2012
Subject: 12-2VM IT1 Case Overviews
(UNCLASSIFIED)

Team Members,

Use the information herein for reference when performing your mission. As always, this is subject to change. I simply want you all to have a good general background on the cases. We will still perform pre/post briefs however. (Confidential Case Numbers have been eliminated.)

9/10 Mar – Case 1165* (Quang Nam Province)
Overview: Looking for site where 1x U.S. Soldier was killed by enemy action.

UNACCOUNTED

(9 May 1968) IVO Hill 352. U.S. Witness, Michael McDonald-Low (1LT/PL) will lead.

11 Mar - Case XXXX (Quang Nam Province)

Overview: Interview witnesses to clarify the disposition of 2x Soldiers. Survey burial locations in garden and quarry.

13 Mar - Case XXXX (Quang Nam Province)

Overview: Interview witness regarding possession of ID Card/disposition of A-4E pilot. Hit and crashed, no observed ejection or pilot (post-crash). This requires expanding survey (50x50m) based on imagery analysis. Need landowner info as well.

14 Mar - Case XXXX (Quang Nam Province)

Overview: Interview witness and conduct survey for remains of Soldier who was injured following parachute drop (1of 4). Found weapon, equipment, spent AK-47 rounds. These 3 witnesses discovered remains at foot of steep slope adjacent to stream and parachute harness; Sep '91 (JFA24).

15 Mar - Case XXXX (Quang Nam Province)

Overview: Interview witnesses and conduct extended 25x25m survey of previous excavated area. UH-1H crashed and pilot could not be extracted. SAR found no body 4-days later. Witness says he buried body next to wreckage 2–days after incident. Witness states that he recovered an ID tag, religious medallion.

16 Mar - Case XXXX (Quang Nam Province)

Overview: Large area based on aircraft crash/personal effects discovery. Canvass and survey for remains, crash, personal effects. This is an A-4E crash (Apr70) (1x unaccounted) w/ proximity to two F-4E's that collided 4-months later.

18 Mar - Case XXXX (Quang Nam Province)

Overview: UH-1C helicopter exploded in midair and fell into A Vuong River Bank (May 68). Patrol located remains of four crewmembers, but they were not recovered. Witness to lead us to this site for a survey.

19 Mar - Case XXXX (Quang Nam Province)

Overview: Survey remains locations on high ledge for the body/personal effects of a Marine who died there (May 68) from frag and gunshot wounds. He was part of a recon patrol and the narrow ledge is said to be near a 300' cliff. We need a higher LZ for this one to work down from.

20 Mar - Case XXXX (Quang Nam Province)

Overview: Search and Rescue attempted to extract dead pilot in body bag from A-1H crash (Jan69) but body fell during hoist.

UNACCOUNTED

These witnesses apparently saw the body being hoisted and it falling into stream.

21 Mar - Case Uncorrelated (Quang Nam Province)
Overview: Canvas locals for information regarding unknown aircraft crash (1968) and aircraft witness Vo reportedly shot down ('67/68). Deconflict, correlate, canvas, interview, and survey.

24 Mar - Case XXXX (Thua Thien-Hue Province)
Overview: Interview AAA company commander (witness) who knows about 3x separate helo crashes. This case is a UH-1D that was hit (Apr 68) resulting in a crewmember being thrown out at 3-4k feet.

25 Mar - Case XXXX (Thua Thien-Hue Province)
Overview: Interview AAA company commander (witness) who knows about 3x separate helo crashes. This case is a CH-47A that was hit (Apr 68) and crashed. Both pilots escaped but there was another ammo explosion and they don't know what happened to the remaining 3x crew members. Record loss was surveyed (JFA32) with negative results.

26 Mar - Case XXXX (Thua Thien-Hue Province)
Overview: Interview AAA company commander (witness) who knows about 3x separate helo crashes. This case is a CH-47A

that was hit (Apr 68) and caught fire. 2x crew jumped out (100 150') and are unaccounted.

27 Mar - Case XXXX (Thua Thien-Hue Province)

Overview: Recon Soldier was hit several times while providing covering fire and body could not be recovered. Witness was member of recon unit that collected U.S. Soldiers MG, watch, and rucksack. They left the body unburied. He was interviewed before and apparently was pretty shaken by the experience and wouldn't take the joint team to the site. Good site sketch.

29 Mar - Case XXXX (Thua Thien-Hue Province)

Overview: Survey location where parachute was located (JFA41/46). We'll need a closer LZ than JFA95, possibly the JFA41 LZ. Pilot and Navigator were forced to eject from their F-4D and were separated on separate sides of hill. Navigator was never recovered. A couple laborers/witnesses discovered flight suit w/ID card while clearing LZ (JFA41) and left it draped over log at stream near a stream. Joint team returned (JFA46) and got the suit, but survey was negative for anything else. *Cut LZ on top of hill.

30 Mar - Case XXXX (Thua Thien-Hue Province)

Overview: Marine was killed while on patrol (Nov 67). Witness said to be our primary has job obligations that have kept him from escorting the joint team previously. Witness health is a concern.

31 Mar - Case XXXX (Thua Thien-Hue Province)

Overview: Looking for AH-1G pilot from a crash (Ma r69) on a ridge. Search and Rescue rescued the other crew member and another team found the pilots helmet and unbuckled seatbelt 2-days later. A previous witness allegedly discovered crash site and possible burial on Da Mong Mountain but could not pinpoint the location during JFA102. His statement during JFA92 was that he found a piece of remains while digging and an ID tag on a chain 50-100m above remains location. His wife allegedly found wreckage higher up the mountain. Witness will lead us to site. Witness apparently sole survivor.

1 Apr - Case XXXX (Thua Thien-Hue Province)

Overview: UH-1H was hit and crashed (Feb 70). 3 of 4 made it back, but POW camp commander showed co-pilot the critically injured pilot's personal effects and told him that he died of wounds and was buried near crash site. Witness couldn't lead the team due to health during JFA95. This is an active rice paddy so we need to ensure that it's ready. Clarify mention of cave or was it "low shallow burial near a stream"?

Summary

18x cases (10 burials, 8 crash sites)

1x U.S. witness (Mr. Michael McDonald-Low)
> Respectfully,
> Favian J. McLaren
> J2, Team Leader/Vietnam IT1

———

EMAIL
Michael McDonald-Low to Ray Carne JPAC J2
24 Feb 2012

Dear Ray,

That is quite a mission line-up.

I will do my best.

I received the new Travel forms and I see I am being sent to Hanoi, while the Team gets their equipment. For someone who has not thought about ever returning to Vietnam this is turning out to be quite a mission.

I want 1165 found. See you next Tuesday.

Michael

———

EMAIL
Carne, Ray Civ JPAC J2 to Michael McDonald-Low
24 Feb 2012

Michael,

The side trip to Hanoi is a great opportunity for you while the gear gets sorted. You'll be met by our Detachment 2 team who are based there.

Ray

Chapter 35

JPAC

Narrative: *M. McDonald-Low*

February 2012

I arrived in Honolulu, Hawaii, on 28 February 2012, at 1310 hours in the afternoon. I came off the airplane in pure "mission" mode. I had finally made it. I was just days away from returning to Vietnam after forty-four years and finally putting an end to the mystery of 1165's location. I felt confident I could find him. I had years of research and I had received the best maps the DoD could supply me. My memory was sharp.

As I walked out of baggage claim I had no idea who was there to greet me until I saw a sign with my name on it held by a female Army staff sergeant dressed in camo fatigues, boots and hat.

As I walked over to her, I paused and said, "I'm the man you're looking for."

"Mr. McDonald-Low, I am Jessica Hernandez with JPAC. Welcome to Hawaii," she said, extending a hand and firm handshake.

I knew from my emails with Jessica that she was a case analyst, active military, and our only female team member. Jess was dark-haired, 5'6" tall, fit, and good-looking even in uniform. She had been to Vietnam on missions several times before and was experienced in Southeast Asia MIA cases. Ray had told me Jessica was a go-getter, a solid soldier, and a real benefit to the IT. She had also been given the unenviable task of being my "witness sitter." In other words, her responsibility was to make sure I was where I was supposed to be and not to lose their only American witness.

"Thanks for picking me up, Jessica. I've looked forward to this for a while. It's good to be here. Thanks for your emails, they were really helpful."

"No problem, Mr. McDonald-Low. Ray Carne sends his best and has asked me to tell you he will pick you up at 0830 tomorrow morning on his way to JPAC. He wants you to just relax, settle in this afternoon, and enjoy being in Hawaii."

Jessica then drove me to the Ilwani Hotel and dropped me off. The Ilwani was close to Hickam Air Force Base as Ray had described, and it was filled with military personnel and their families. It was apparently one of those "in and out" transit hotels that saw a number of service people coming and going. It fit my needs, and I settled in and relaxed. It had been a long flight from California on a morning that began for me at 0600 hours. I was glad to be in Hawaii, but apprehensive about the mission ahead. I had never wanted to return to Vietnam, and here I was just days from doing exactly that. 1165 was on my mind.

The next morning, 1 March, after two years of emails and phone calls, I finally met Ray Carne as I walked out of the hotel. Ray, a Thai by birth, grew up in Hawaii. He was forty-eight years old, 5'8" tall, and had black hair, a medium build, broad face, and a large smile filled with white teeth. Ray was dressed "island style," with a flower print shirt and khaki trousers.

"Michael. It's about time," Ray said as he walked up to me, shook my hand and patted me on the back. "Welcome to Hawaii and Mission 12-2VM."

"It's really good to be here, Ray. It's a real pleasure to meet you in person," I said, with a big smile on my face. "I can't believe I'm actually here. It's been a long time."

Ray looked stressed as we loaded into his car, a white four-door Chevy sedan. I asked him, "Ray, what's going on? Everything still a go?"

"Yes, no problem. As you know, we've got eighteen IT missions scheduled, and they leave in three days. We also have some recovery teams going and that's in the same timetable. I'm just busy with the details, it's all good. I'm excited for you to see JPAC and meet your team members of IT-1."

As we drove to and entered Hickam AFB, Ray informed me that the JPAC command was activated Oct. 1, 2003, and was currently employing more than 500 joint military and civilian personnel. The JPAC facilities were housed in military-style, metal Quonset buildings, older wooden barracks, and a few small warehouses.

Overall, Hickam AFB and the JPAC Command were exactly what I remembered of military posts on Hawaii from the 60s. Most of the buildings were constructed prior to WWII and Pearl Harbor. There'd been many coats of paint since then, but they were essentially the same as when they were built.

Ray took me to his office after showing me around the JPAC grounds. It was an eighty-foot long Quonset style metal building that had been portioned off into cubicles. Ray's desk sat behind a partition in the middle. His walls were covered with maps, photos of former JPAC members, and memorabilia of their missions.

As I sat down opposite his desk, Ray admired the hat I'd been wearing. "I knew I needed to have headgear Ray, and I thought this hat I had made was perfect." It was a black baseball-style cap, pro model, and fitted. On the lower right front was written "ELEVEN SIXTY-FIVE," and on the lower left side of the hat was written "12-2VM." Next to the mission number on the left front, I had my original brass crossed rifles, and next to it was a small replica crest of the 11th Light Infantry Brigade. It was the hat I intended to wear every day, especially in Vietnam.

"I am not going to hide who I am while I'm there, Ray, not even in Hanoi."

"Mike, it looks great. I think it's appropriate. The crossed rifles are a nice touch. The brigade pin as well."

"Thanks. I'm glad you like it," I said, as I reached into the backpack I had with me. I pulled out an identical hat, without the crossed rifle or pin, and presented it to Ray. "I thought you could use your own, my friend."

"Very nice. Very cool. And it's just my size," he said trying it on. Ray had a small window behind his cubicle and he looked at his reflection.

"Mike, that is so nice of you. Thanks, again. I'll keep it as a keepsake of the mission. I wanted to tell you how important you are to our mission. It's rare that we get an American witness; I think you may be the fifth. It really helps us to set the record straight when we have someone who was there at the incident and knows where he's going."

Ray then escorted me out of his cubicle. As we walked around the corner to another office he explained to me,

"You're going to meet our Southeast Asia department head, Bob Masters, or as we like to call him 'Bulldog' or 'Bad Bob.' Bob has been here since he originally began as a forensic anthropologist on our JPAC Investigative teams in the mid-2000s. He has years of experience and good success, because once he gets his teeth into a case, he won't let go. He's tenacious about the MIA cause and getting them home."

We entered the small office and, as we did, Bob Masters came over to me and looked me up and down. He then shook my hand aggressively. Bob was slight of build, about 5'8", and had graying fair hair and a closely cropped gray beard that seemed to accent his hawk-like features. I immediately sensed why this man had the "bulldog" nickname.

"Real good to see you, Mr. Low. I've read your notes and information about 1165, good stuff. I am very pleased to have you on board," Masters said, as he finished shaking my hand.

He then turned to Ray and said, "Ray, before you introduce Mr. Low to the team, I'd like you to brief him on the history of JPAC. I've got meetings with the staff, and I will catch up with you both tomorrow."

Although Masters was immediately welcoming and friendly, there was an underlying demeanor to him that carried the "don't screw with me" label. Not a large man, he was aggressive in his speech and movement. Bob then nodded to us both as we left his office, politely dismissed.

Ray took me back to his cubicle, pulled out their official JPAC briefing sheet, and then told me how JPAC all started. "JPAC really first began in 1973 as the Central Identification Laboratory-Thailand, and it was focused exclusively on the Americans missing in Southeast Asia. In 1976, the Central Identification Laboratory-Hawaii was established to search for, recover, and identify missing Americans from all previous conflicts. That was the full extent of the POW/MIA effort. It had never been done prior to Vietnam for any conflict. It was the Vietnam Moms who really made the formation of the Central Identification Laboratory happen."

"In 1992, the government formed the Joint Task Force-Full Accounting (JFA) to focus on achieving the fullest possible accounting of Americans missing as a result of the Vietnam War. In 2002, the Department of Defense determined that the POW/MIA efforts would be best served by combining both Central Identification Laboratory organizations and the Joint Task Force-Full Accounting. In late 2003, the Joint POW/MIA Accounting Command (JPAC) was formed to search for all U.S. combatants from all wars. I've been here since then and our mission today is unchanged. We want them all home."

Ray further explained to me that the core of JPAC's day-to-day operations involves researching case files, investigating leads, excavating sites and identifying Americans who were killed in action but were never brought home. The process involves close coordination with U.S. agencies involved in the POW/MIA issue, including the Defense Prisoner of War/Missing Personnel Office, Catherine's office, the Armed Forces Mortuary Affairs Offices, U. S. Pacific Command, Department of State, the Joint Staff, Defense Intelligence Agency, the Armed Forces DNA Identification Laboratory, and the U.S. Air Force's Life Sciences Equipment Laboratory.

"We are also routinely engaged in negotiations and talks with representatives of foreign governments to promote and maintain positive in-country conditions wherever our teams deploy. Such is the case with 1165, Mike. We've been working with the government of the Socialist Republic of Vietnam, and they will be providing assistance to you and your Investigative Team."

"What? I wasn't expecting an NVA escort, Ray," I said to him.

"We couldn't do what we do without them. In fact, it's the only way we can conduct a search in Vietnam. The country would never allow just anyone to come over and start poking around and looking for a missing American. They are very strict about that type of thing. Of course, the other motivator is the money. Each investigation is very costly. The government of Vietnam is paid very well to assist us."

Referring to his JPAC briefing sheet, Ray went on to explain that the search for unaccounted-for American soldiers starts with in-depth research by JPAC historians and analysts. These experts gather information from records, archives, interviews, and other sources. In most cases, the search for a missing person will involve outside researchers, the national archives, and record depositories maintained by the U.S. and foreign governments. Veterans, external historians, private citizens, families of missing Americans, and amateur researchers also routinely provide information about cases.

"We take this information and create a 'loss incident case file' for each unaccounted individual. This case file includes historical background, military medical and personnel records, unit histories, official correspondence, maps, photographs, and other evidence. This groundwork lays the foundation to locate possible sites where missing Americans may be located.

After evidence and information is gathered, JPAC sends out an investigation team to potential sites. Each team consists of four to nine people including a team leader, analyst, linguist, communication technician, and medic. In some instances, an anthropologist, explosive ordnance disposal technician, forensic photographer, and life support technician may augment the team.

That's what your IT-1 team will be like. We have a full complement of experts to assist you with 1165. In total, there will be twelve. And they are dedicated and anxious to work with you, Mike. An American Witness is special and rare to accompany our teams there. Most times, we don't have the kind of information that you will be providing, it's usually all second hand. It's a great help to have you on board."

"Thank you, Ray. It's a real honor for me to help. I believe 1165 has been there long enough."

"There's no doubt about that, my friend. Now, let me show you our lab. When we are lucky and skilled enough to get an accurate location of a missing soldier, our recovery teams excavate the site under the close supervision of our archeologist. If during the course of the search any materials that we suspect are from a missing soldier, they are transported to our Central Identification Laboratory for analysis. The Central Identification Laboratory is the largest and most diverse forensic skeletal laboratory in the world."

The Lab was impressive, as was the entire facility. I was particularly fascinated with the glass showcases that lined the exterior of the lab. The cases were filled with photos and memorabilia from successful JPAC searches. There were dog tags, rusted weapons, pictures of JPAC teams rappelling into remote cliff sides, photos of burned-out helicopters and jets crashed in remote jungles, and sample artifacts from various sites. It was grim, mesmerizing, and for me, hopeful.

Chapter 36

THE MISSION TEAM
Narrative: *M. McDonald-Low*
March 2012

I was introduced to Major General Thomas, the commanding general of JPAC, at our scheduled appointment time of 1600 hours.

Major General Stephan Thomas greeted me in his office and, for the next thirty minutes, we visited privately about JPAC and specifically 1165. A soft-spoken, highly educated man of Asian descent, General Thomas was personable and engaging. He had reviewed the brief on 1165 that I had prepared for my JPAC Team.

"Mr. McDonald-Low, the document you prepared was very detailed and informative. I am particularly interested in how 1165 came to be misidentified and lost for so long. I read the document, but please tell me your account."

He listened carefully as I explained the unusual circumstances that surrounded 1165's loss, and how he was reported killed on a different day and location. He was also highly cognizant of the previous JPAC missions that had searched unsuccessfully for 1165.

"I don't believe we have that to contend with any longer. I am very confident that with your inclusion and information, we are well on our way to finding 1165."

General Thomas then rose and shook my hand, "The best of luck on your mission."

When he shook my hand, he passed me his personal "Challenge Coin" that was marked with his two star insignia and "Commander JPAC" on one side and the JPAC logo and motto on the other. I accepted the coin and felt very honored and privileged to have received it.

"Thanks so much, General. I am very grateful for all of the support and your kind words."

"You're welcome, Mr. McDonald-Low. Thank you. I'll be seeing you again when you and your team get ready to depart on March 3rd." I was dismissed.

I walked back to Ray's office and along the way, I found myself in high spirits. I felt buoyed by my meeting with General Thomas and anxious to meet the other members of my team.

Ray first introduced me to Dr. C. Elliot Johanson, our team archeologist. I quickly learned that everyone called Dr. Johanson, "Hoss," and he was quite a character. Imagine a larger, mid-60s, heavier Indiana Jones with a droopy mustache. A big man with an even bigger personality, Hoss looked the part of the "jungle adventurer archeologist." He always wore a broad brimmed hat turned down rakishly in the front, long sleeved shirts with the sleeves rolled up, a loose fitting "GI style" neck wrap, khaki trousers held up by suspenders, and hiking boots.

Hoss was born deaf, but he could read lips in multiple languages, including Vietnamese. He had been to Vietnam on forty-five previous missions and was a virtual encyclopedia on the Vietnam War. He always referred to the NVA or VC as "Charley." As I was to learn, he loved telling stories and sharing his knowledge gained from his many trips to Vietnam. He also had the endearing habit of speaking at full volume, virtually all of the time.

Favian McLaren was our team leader. Favian was a chief warrant officer in Intelligence and had been on many JPAC missions. Muscular, round faced, and in his 30s, Favian was 5'10" tall, brown-haired and serious about his job. Soft spoken, I could tell by his demeanor that he was the man in-charge. I was also lucky to meet him, as he was originally scheduled to leave for Vietnam earlier, but his plans were changed at the last minute.

Kerry Pike was a five-tour Middle East veteran and a Special Forces medic. He was there to make sure I didn't expire on the trip, and to treat any injuries should they occur to our team. A big, handsome guy, Kerry was 6'3" tall, mustached and had close-cropped, light brown hair that was graying just about everywhere. He typified the Special Ops soldier: tough, professional and reliable.

David Clark was also in the military, having recently returned from Afghanistan where he was an EOD specialist. Dave was in his late 20s, about 5'10" tall, dark-haired with boyish good looks. Dave was with us to locate and disarm any ordinance we may run across, and to apply his metal-detecting skills in the search. Dave's recent Middle East tour had left him with a nerve condition that discolored his hands with reddish and white splotches. I thought it was an indication of just how stressful it could be being a bomb specialist.

Wes Martin was assigned as my case analyst. It would be his job to document the mission, as well as supervising any search activities and interviews. Wes was hard to figure out because he never said much. He looked like he could be Favian's brother; both at 5'10" tall, brown-haired, stocky, rounder-faced, and current military.

I would later meet our two interpreters/analysts, Hieu Trang and Phong Huen, as well as Paul Villasa, our official mission photographer, and Howard Munson and Clint Button, both case analysts. Jessica, my "sitter," was off working on her personal packing for the next day's official mission equipment loading.

After I had met everyone present, Ray wanted to introduce me to "Sanctuary." "Sanctuary" was located just outside Ray's office, past the parking lot in a small, secluded grotto. There was a sign that hung on the entrance, and there were flowers and greenery surrounding a bamboo bar, picnic style tables, and barbecue. Ray showed me the wall behind the bar where it was covered with pictures of people from various missions.

"This is our place, Mike. Those pictures are on what we call the 'Wall of Honor.' 'Sanctuary' is where missions are discussed, victories celebrated, and where the memories of MIAs are held close and revered."

I was honored to be there.

Chapter 37

UP, UP, AND AWAY

Narrative: *M. McDonald-Low*

March 2012

The next day and a half I spent with the JPAC mission personnel as they prepared to leave. Just loading the gear was a challenge. All of their equipment had to be placed into giant metal containers and pallets that would then be hauled to and loaded aboard a giant USAF C-17 Globemaster.

Some teams would be in country as long as forty-five days and required a variety of supplies, tools, and apparatus for the complex areas they would visit and the searches they would conduct. The search areas were as varied as the landscape of Vietnam and included mountains, jungles, forests, river deltas, and all points in between. Some were habited, most were remote. It was no surprise that they traveled with such a load.

One of the things my teammates, especially Jessica, impressed upon me was how to prepare for the flight to Vietnam. The C-17 Globemaster was not at all like a civilian jet airliner. The C-17 was going to be cold in-flight and the flight was long. Everyone would be bringing sleeping pads, air mattresses and gear for sleeping on the floor. The seats were military sling-style and were not designed for comfort or sleeping.

I wasn't concerned. I had months of time to prepare and I knew what to bring. I was anxious to get going and relieved when at 2130 hours, 3 March, we reached the small airport area at Hickam's Air Force terminal and prepared to leave. General Thomas and his wife showed up to send us on our way and wish us well, as did my good buddy, Ray. It was a perfect send-off.

The Globemaster was a huge, cavernous plane. Dark gray with black markings, its wings stretched and drooped as the giant twin jet engines gaped at me with their huge black intakes. The cockpit windows looked tiny and seemed to tower above me. As I walked up the ramp and through the door, I saw that down each side of the plane were nylon-strapped seats, which sat against the bare metal frame and outer wall of the aircraft. There was also a short row of back-to-back outward facing seats that ran down the middle in the front half of the aircraft. The already loaded giant pallets of gear occupied most of the middle and rear of the aircraft and were strapped down tight to the rollers on the aircraft floor that assisted in pallet loading.

I sat down and strapped in, Jessica on one side and Favian on the other. Everyone else grabbed their seats and strapped in as well.

Jess leaned in next to me and said with a slight smile, "This is it. We are on our way to the promised land."

"To be honest, Jess, I have never wanted to return to Vietnam. It's the last place on my travel destination list. I believed I had seen everything there I wanted." It was the story I had told so many times I thought it was almost true; "ain't no big thang" was still with me in spirit.

The giant jets whirred as each engine spun up to speed and the plane began to slowly taxi. I was glad the noise had interrupted my conversation with Jess. At long last I was finally getting started on my journey to find 1165, and it was what I was focused upon.

The big Globemaster rolled, gathered speed, and roared into the night of Hawaii. First stop was Anderson AFB, Guam, 4,000 miles and nine hours away.

As soon as the big jet reached its cruising altitude, the JPAC teams unstrapped and grabbed their positions on the floor. I grabbed a spot next to the front of the pallets, laid out my air mattress and "woobie," and settled in for the long journey. I mainly slept and read the whole way or talked with Favian and Jessica about the 1165 document I had given each of them. The flight was cold, but not unbearable, and seemed to pass quickly. We touched down in Guam at 0130 hours, March 4.

While the big jet was being refueled, we received a random bus ride down the base past some Global Hawks that were in on stand-down. We learned from our escort that the Northrop Grumman RQ-4 Global Hawk is an unmanned aerial vehicle (UAV) surveillance aircraft. In role and operational design, the Global Hawk is similar to the Lockheed U-2 spy plane, with long loiter times over target areas, it can survey as much as 40,000 square miles of terrain a day.

The Global Hawk was impressive and weird looking. It had a strangely bent fuselage with a big jet motor strapped to its back between two, large tail wings. It had a big head in the front where the cockpit would be, but there were no windows. Its wings were not particularly long and it looked somewhat awkward, while being very space age in appearance.

After our brief tour of the "Hawks" we boarded our Globemaster and lifted off into the early morning for our next destination, Phuket, Thailand, 2739 miles and eight hours away. A replica of our first tour leg, everyone camped out on the floor and tried to sleep, read or talk with their teammates quietly. I did the same, but I also received a treat being invited up to the cockpit to meet the pilots and crew.

"Up" was the real description, as the cockpit sat well above everything else in the huge cargo bay. As I climbed up the steps and entered the door to the cockpit I didn't expect it to be so big and utilitarian. Six large windows sat above clusters and banks of gauges, navigation screens, and radios. The two Air Force pilots sat opposite each other about six feet apart, separated by handles and flight controls. Immediately behind the pilots were two additional seats for the navigation officer and crew chief. The pilots looked barely in their twenties, but I learned from our conversations they were both highly experienced and had made this trip many times.

We landed in Phuket, Thailand, at about 1300 hours, 4 March. We would spend the afternoon and evening there with a departure of 0900 hours the next morning. I felt like I had been flying forever as we checked into our beach side hotel. It was a beautiful place, but I was so tired from the eighteen hours of flying, I hardly noticed as I grabbed a quick lunch at the hotel restaurant and headed to my room for a shower and a nap. It felt good to be on the ground and great to be in Thailand. One more stop and I'd be there.

My "nap" lasted twelve hours. My JPAC teammates must have felt the same way, because I caught several of them in the elevator headed to the lobby looking for food the next morning at 0700 hours. We were due to be aboard and in the air within the next two hours.

Chapter 38

Narrative: *M. McDonald-Low*
5 March 2012

I landed in Danang, Vietnam, at 1120 hours, 5 March 2012, at the same airport I left from in 1968. It had been forty-four years and a lifetime ago. I sat quietly in my seat as the C-17 finally rolled to a stop.

Jessica looked over at me, smiled, and quietly said, "You have waited a long time for this and you're here. This is your moment."

I was nervous, hesitant, and at the same time, positively anxious. I breathed a sigh of relief and gathered myself. My heart was pounding like the many times I had startled myself awake from my dreams. The dream was now ending. At long last, I had what I wanted and didn't, all at the same time.

My other teammates and members of the other JPAC teams all stood as I was directed to the front of the plane. I was to be the first one down the ramp. Favian McLaren stood by the inside of the door and shook my hand. He looked at me as he held my hand and said, "This has been a long journey for you. I am happy to be here and I assure you we will do everything we can to help your mission be a success. Welcome back to Vietnam."

I then walked out and down the ramp into the bright sunshine of Vietnam.

It was quiet. I could hear my footsteps on the metal ramp leading down to the tarmac. For the first time I heard Vietnam without the distant thunder of B-52s, or the rumble of concussions from heavy artillery pounding the nearby mountains. No slicks sat in neat rows on the apron of the strip or dotted the horizon in formations of six or nine, and no gunships protectively circled the airport, the thwop-thwop of their blades now a forgotten memory.

The airport terminal looked relatively new. It wasn't large and was comparable in size to many U.S. suburban and commuter airports. I stood there, wondering where I was. For a moment I had visions of being at the Sacramento Airport.

Just as I was admiring the quiet and stillness, I saw and then heard four military jets roar their way down the runway past us, two strips over.

"Mike, they're just showing off. They do it every time we land. I guess it's their idea of showing us who's boss here. You know Charley hasn't changed much, Mike. Lots of bravado and hurrah," said Hoss, as he walked up beside me and watched the jets head off into the horizon, their contrails white against the blue sky.

Hoss then leaned in to me and said loudly, "That's our escort team over there by the Customs door, Mike. They'll be with us the entire time and will drive us. The tallest of the four is the major. We've been with him before. The other three are just drivers and his assistants. They're just here to help. The major is here to help us too, but he is also an intelligence officer and observes and reports everything we do to their government. It's all about the money. They charge the United States Government for every mile we drive, every interview we take, every tree and bush we disturb. Everything. One more thing, he says he doesn't speak English, but we all know better. He is Charley, the 21st Century version, Mike. Smart mother fucker. Don't underestimate him."

I looked at the major as Hoss explained to me that he was our escort and official "guide." The major was a thin, dark-haired Asian about 5'9" tall, and he had angular, sharply defined features. He was dressed casually, as were his three Vietnamese assistants, whom I thought of as "Huey, Duey, and Louie."

As we retrieved our baggage from one of the pallets, my IT-1 teammates and I headed for Customs, which was a mere formality as we had all been pre-approved by the Socialist

Government for our journey. The major and his men waited for us outside the Customs building beside four Mitsubishi, four-door, 4WD Pajero land cruisers. Each of the cruisers carried two red flags with a yellow star in the middle. The flags were mounted on each side of their front bumper. The rear doors of each were swung up and open so we could load our luggage.

Hoss, Jessica, and I loaded our gear into Huey's cruiser, while the rest of the team split up to the other trucks. I saw that Favian was riding with the major, one of our interpreters, and Wes Martin.

I had never seen Danang other than as a war base, so I didn't really know what to expect as we began our thirty-minute drive to a downtown hotel. We were to spend the day and night in Danang, and then the team would depart the next morning for our mission base at Tam Ky, while I would be headed for Hanoi.

The ride through the countryside from the airport was effortless, as our red flagged vehicles separated the throngs of scooters, mini-cars, and buses like a hot knife through butter. As we approached the city, I saw more young people and businessmen dressed in modern, fashionable attire. This was unlike many of the people on the outskirts of the city I observed, who still clung to the traditional garb of pajama like clothing and conical straw/thatch "coolie" hats, which many of the women still wore. Vietnam had definitely changed. The downtown buildings and skyscrapers of Danang looked as modern as any U.S. city of that size.

We arrived at the Green Plaza Hotel, a thirty-story modern high rise on the Han River. I had just checked-in and was walking to the elevators to take me to my room when Jessica tapped me on the shoulder. "Don't forget we have our first formal dinner this evening hosted by the major. We're all to meet him promptly in the lobby at 1900 hours."

Jessica then laughed and said, "Make sure you bring your drinking shoes, there will be plenty of formal toasting tonight during the Cuoc Loi ceremonies, and don't forget you've got a flight in the morning to Hanoi."

I wondered what Cuoc Loi was, but my head was still filled with my fresh impressions of Vietnam and thoughts of my forthcoming trip to Hanoi that all I could do was nod at her and say, "Okay."

I went to my room and looked out the windows from the twentieth floor down upon a city at peace. I was really having trouble wrapping my head around what I was seeing. Other than the excess number of scooters, Danang resembled any modern American city. Situated on the coast of the South China Sea, at the mouth of the Han River, Danang was busy and bustling.

I then heard a knock on my door. It was Hoss, and he was hungry. "Come on, Mike let's go get a burger and see the sights. You haven't been to Danang for a long time."

"I think you're absolutely right, Hoss. I was just standing and looking out the window and thinking how much everything has changed. It'd be good to see it up close, and I've always wanted a burger in downtown Danang," I replied facing him so he could read my lips. I was also smiling.

I grabbed my sunglasses and we rode the elevator to the Green Plaza lobby. We walked out of the hotel onto the sidewalk and looked up and down the street. The street in front of the hotel had an expansive concrete boardwalk along the riverfront that stretched as far as I could see. Artisans, vendors, tourists, and locals crowded the boardwalk. We joined them and strolled through the many displays and goods that ranged from small tourist ware and jewelry, to life sized, hand-chiseled statuaries of horses and dolphins, to modern electronics that included iPads and cell phones.

Hoss remarked to me as we stopped to look at the hotels, restaurants, and businesses along the river, "Mike, this is what happens when you give a poor economy money. It prospers. Isn't it interesting that most of this success you see here is from American dollars? Charley has done very well for himself since the war."

I smiled at Hoss's reference to Charley, "Apparently so, Hoss. This boardwalk could be in San Diego."

"That's true, but remember, Vietnam at its core is no different than when you left. I'll show you a market that is more of what you may remember."

Hoss then guided me to the Danang Farmers Market, which he assured me would be entertaining and one of the biggest and most varied I'd see. It was.

The market was housed in an older, multi-story building that sat opposite the boardwalk on the other side of the street. The bottom floor of the building was open-ended and filled from one end to the other with small booths featuring vendors selling their fruits, vegetables, clothing, hats, watches, and souvenirs. Many of the vendors were dressed in peasant garb and looked no different than the Vietnamese we used to encounter in small villages in 1968.

It was both strange and familiar.

Strangest of all and my favorite were the Ruou Thuoc, or "medicine wines" with cobras, venomous black scorpions, and bamboo viper green snakes beautifully mounted in yellow bottles filled with wine.

Each yellow bottle had an elaborately staged cobra attacking a green snake or a scorpion. They were so professionally mounted each looked like fine sculptures. I learned from Hoss that the cobras used to make the snake wine had their poison cancelled out by the alcoholic content of the drink. Similarly, months of fermenting meant the dead scorpions encased in the yellow bottles didn't have the same sting in their tail as when they were alive.

Hoss knew all about the wines and gave me his scientific explanation, "Mike, it's quite simple actually. Snake venoms are protein-based, but they are inactivated by the denaturing effects of ethanol and are rendered harmless. The liquor is considered to have many health benefits."

"Oh, I bet they do. Nothing like good ol' snake wine to get you through the night!" I said laughing, as I held one of the bottles.

Hoss, undeterred by my sarcasm, continued, "Snake and scorpion wines are considered natural medicines and are used to treat back pain, rheumatism, lumbago, and other health conditions. However, the real reason for their popularity is that these rice-based liquors are also considered to be strong natural aphrodisiacs."

I laughed again, and as I held up the bottle I said, "Viagra in a bottle. Snakes and scorpions included for extra sting. Good stuff!"

"If you're interested in taking one home, you're out of luck. Ruou Thuoc is illegal in the U.S.," Hoss said laughing.

"I think I am good to go without the wine, big man. How about that cheeseburger you promised me?"

A cheeseburger in Danang, Vietnam? It seemed hard to believe.

Tam's Cheeseburger Bar sat virtually across the street from the Farmers Market and was positioned near the hotel for obvious reasons. The interior was about twelve by twenty-five feet and it had a small wood bar that had stools provided for seating. I could see through two, small swinging doors that the kitchen was in the back. A menu in English and Vietnamese offered burgers, fries, and beer. I wasn't disappointed. The cheeseburger was excellent, and it again reminded me how much Vietnam had changed.

Hoss and I returned to the hotel. I went to my room to rest, shower and prepare for my first formal dinner with the major and the infamous Cuoc Loi ceremony.

At 1900 hours, we met the major and his three-man crew at a private restaurant down the street from the hotel. The restaurant sign said closed, but the owner was waiting out front to greet us. I could also see a few other people waiting inside the glass entrance doors. The restaurant would be open exclusively for us that evening. Apparently the major had his connections.

Chapter 39

FACE TO FACE

Narrative: *M. McDonald–Low*

5 March 2012

As we stood in front of the restaurant, I was formally introduced to the major. Major Nguyen Thien shook my hand and said in clear English, "Welcome to Vietnam, Mister Mike." He then gestured to Phong, our interpreter, and spoke to him in rapid-fire Vietnamese.

Phong listened carefully to the major and then said to me, "The major wishes you well on your mission. He also says he has brought a special guest for you this evening."

Guest? My first reaction was one of disbelief. I knew the major was familiar with my background because my mission was contained in a brief that was vetted by them prior to my coming to Vietnam. The major knew as much as I did about my mission to find 1165.

I walked into the restaurant following the major and my JPAC team. We paused after arriving in the foyer and then a small Vietnamese man walked up to me. He was dressed in green khakis and wearing a green, military-style soft hat with a gold star. He stopped right in front of me, smiling. He then reached up and touched my nearly white goatee. As he did, with a broad smile he lifted his hat and ran his fingers through his snow-white hair. He smiled again and spoke to me in Vietnamese. Phong was standing nearby and translated, "It is good to see an old soldier from the American War. Time has treated you well. Welcome."

I didn't know what to say, but I struggled with, "It's good to meet you, too."

I was thinking about his phrase the "American War," when Phong leaned into the small man again and listened. He then turned back to me and said, "This man's name is Ling Pho. He is a former NVA infantry officer, captain with the 2nd NVA Division, 3rd Regiment. He fought against you in 1968. He has a wealth of memories from that time, and he wishes to share and compare them with you tonight."

I was incredulous. Meeting an NVA I fought against, and then having dinner with him was something I had never conceived in my wildest dreams. Why would I?

We were then guided to a room that had two large circular tables that were prepared for the seventeen of us. I was seated next to Ling Pho on my right, with Phong just seated to his right. On my left were my good buddies Hoss, Jessica, and Favian. Across the table I saw Kerry nod to me. Ever ominous because of his size and demeanor, he was my physical watchdog and took the job seriously. Even when dressed in a Hawaiian print shirt, as he was tonight, Kerry looked like he was just waiting to kick some ass.

The evening began as soon as everyone was seated. The major gestured to Huey, who nodded to Louie, and a waiter brought in four large, corked-glass bottles and sat them in front of the major. The waiter opened a bottle and filled a small, shot-sized glass with a stem bottom. The major smelled it, and then tasted it. He nodded approvingly around to the two tables, smiled, and said with deep inflection, "Cuoc Loi!"

Two more waiters entered the room and immediately began filling everyone's Cuoc Loi mini-goblets.

The major had remained standing and waiting for the glasses to be filled. Everyone then stood with full glasses in hand. I had already been warned by Jess that the custom was all people participating in the toast must drink their drink as the toaster did.

The major then lifted his glass and said in clear accent-free English, "Welcome to Vietnam and good success." He then tossed back the Cuoc Loi in one gulp. We all followed suit.

Cuoc Loi tastes like a cross between vodka and wine, and it has a burn. I had no idea what the potency was, but it definitely had a kick.

I had taken my seat when I felt a tap on my shoulder. Ling Pho then stood next to me with a full shot of Cuoc Loi and with a broad smile, he gestured for me to stand. A waiter approached and quickly filled my glass. Ling Pho then said something in Vietnamese, raised glass and saluted me with it before downing the contents. I smiled and did the same, looking at Phong for a translation.

Phong said, "Mr. Pho has officially toasted to your health and your good fortune in surviving the war."

"Tell Mr. Pho thank you. It's an honor to meet with a soldier from the 2nd NVA Division, 3rd Regiment. They were a very tough unit."

Pho rattled off a quick response and Phong said, "Mr. Pho says your unit, the 11th Brigade and the 198th were both formidable. Very hard in battle."

I smiled and nodded, and then requested the waiter to come fill Pho's and my glass again. We toasted each other by nodding and saluting with our glasses. We both then sat down and let the conversations at the table absorb us.

It had been strange to hear Ling Pho call it the "American War," but not as unexpected as the first question he asked me when we had started eating our meal of broiled fish, vegetables, rice and noodles. "Do you suffer from PTSD?" Pho asked with Phong's assistance.

I practically choked. I had never in a million years thought of what their soldiers may have experienced. I had always viewed the "Vietnam War" entirely from my perspective.

After recovering from my shock, I told Pho with Phong's help, "Yes, many soldiers including myself have PTSD."

He nodded his head solemnly. "How long did you serve in Vietnam?"

"I was here in 1967 and 1968."

"I spent eight years fighting here in the South; 1966 to 1974. I did not see my family the entire time. They lived in Haiphong, which is far north."

It made me pause, and I thought about how long eight years was in a war like ours. It gave me new respect for the tough little man sitting next to me.

After our meal and many toasts, Pho and I discussed our time together as opponents in the Que Son Valley. He particularly remembered the battle of Hill 352, Nui Hoac Ridge. "It was during the time of what you referred to as our "Mini-Tet" offensive. My unit had learned much in the previous months during our advances on Hue and Danang during our New Year's invasion of the South, (Tet Offensive). We knew the Hiep Duc and Que Son Valley very well. Many of our regimental units had been located there for years. We also knew the Americans would be very determined in their resistance when we launched our attacks. It was a difficult battle."

"Yes, it was. We lost hundreds of men there," I said solemnly looking at him.

He shook his head slowly and said to me, "Where you lost hundreds, we lost thousands."

I looked at him and thought of the perspective. There was no hint of anger or animosity in either of our recollections; they were just memories of old men reminiscing about the hard facts of war from two different sides.

The Cuoc Loi toasts and conversations continued around the table, and as the dinner drew to a close, Ling Pho wished me success on my mission. He then offered me some last words as we walked out of the restaurant, "Many of us on both sides made this journey of war we discussed and some survived. It is good that you and I did. I am glad I celebrated with you the memories of those who did not. Enjoy your trip to our capital tomorrow. Hanoi is very beautiful."

I shook the small man's hand, "Thank you. I wish you a safe journey home, too. It was very special to spend this time with you."

As I walked away with Hoss, Kerry, and the members of my team, returning to the hotel, I thought of what Pho said and I smiled to myself. It had been a most welcome surprise and had made me feel that this trip was going to be a rewarding one. I also had the feeling it was just one of many unexpected things yet in store for me.

After saying goodnight to most of the team, Hoss, Favian, Kerry, and I walked down the street from the Green Plaza to an outdoor bistro just down the block. We chose the only empty table on the sidewalk. The table had a great view of the boardwalk across the street. The night was busy and noisy with scooters and taxis on the busy waterfront. Many Vietnamese couples and young people were also out enjoying the cool night as they walked next to the Han River.

We each ordered beers and just after they arrived, a group of six Vietnamese in their early twenties approached our table. There were four young women and two guys, and all were dressed in modern, western clothing. The men were in jeans and casual shirts, while the girls were in skirts and blouses. They were very excited, happy, and confident, and obviously were out enjoying the nightlife of downtown Danang. One of the young men stepped out front of his companions, and as the girls giggled and talked in the background, he said to us in broken English, "Hello. Are you Americans? My friends and I would very much like to say hello."

Kerry, Hoss, and I looked at each other as Favian stood up and replied in that leadership voice of his, "Yes, we are. We would be most pleased to say hello to you and your friends."

By then we had all gotten to our feet and began introducing ourselves, which sent a shockwave of giggles through the girls. As I suspected, they were all in their early twenties and worked downtown as office workers. They all remarked that they rarely had the opportunity to see or talk with Americans, though it was not considered as rare as it was when they were children.

Each of us in turn was asked where we were from with the states of California and New York getting the biggest reactions. The girls in particular were curious about how "modern" California was and how they would love to see it one day. When they said they especially wanted to visit Hollywood, I had to smile. Tourists.

The guys liked New York and were curious about modern city life and how much money people made. They were also very interested in cars and motorcycles; no big surprise, they were like young men everywhere.

Our visit and conversations with our newly found friends concluded with picture taking, as each wanted a photo with our group. As we said our goodbyes, I could only think of how happy and excited these young Vietnamese were, and how novel our presence was to them. In reality, their parents would have a hard time remembering when Americans were last here.

Hanoi was on my mind.

Chapter 40

HANOI

Narrative: *M. McDonald-Low*
6-7 March 2012

The next morning the major drove me to the Danang airport for my trip to Hanoi. He was quiet and polite during the trip and when we said our goodbyes, he wished me a safe journey. He also told me that a car would be waiting for me at the airport the next afternoon to transport me to the hotel our team was staying at in Tam Ky.

As I entered the airport, I was thinking that Hanoi was probably the last place on earth that I had ever wanted to visit. In the back of my mind, I still considered it to be the "home of the enemy."

After a short flight of just ninety minutes I arrived in Hanoi. As I walked out of the airport I was greeted by a Vietnamese man neatly dressed in a suit, holding a sign with my name on it. He spoke little English other than to convey to me that he was taking me to JPAC's Detachment 2, where I would be staying.

The modern highway from the airport passed from the countryside to the city very quickly. The closer we came to the metropolis of Hanoi, I saw more and more scooters and small trucks. People were on the move. The city itself was very old, and the buildings reflected their past French influence. One of the odd things I noticed was the electrical and telephone lines. The large bundles of black lines that passed from pole to pole and from building to building were about three feet in diameter. The lines were like "spaghetti" as they randomly wound from one connection to another.

As we came to the center of the city, it was about 1000 hours and the roads were packed. At any given stop light, twenty to forty scooters would be massed, six and eight wide on the street. Pedestrians crossed from one side to the other, fearlessly passing between the traffic, even as the light turned green.

Detachment 2 was located behind a walled compound in the middle of where many foreign embassies are located in downtown Hanoi. Officially known to the Socialist Republic of Vietnam as the U.S. MIA Office, Det. 2 is manned by seven, full-time Americans. There are two officers, two enlisted personnel, and three civilians.

After settling into my apartment at the compound, I was taken on a brief walking tour of Hanoi as we headed out to an early lunch. Sergeant's Pope and McKinney were my guides, both having been at Det. 2 for the past fifteen months. I was desperate for some "American" food, especially after having a burger at Tam's. The sergeants assured me that this would be no problem and they were right.

Stopping at a fashionable, but small restaurant, I was amazed to see the place packed with foreigners, but after looking at the menu, I knew why. My dreams had come true, real food; steaks, burgers, potatoes (not rice), ribs, and green salads were the highlights.

As we waited for our orders, the two sergeants told me that during my visit at Det. 2, the staff had arranged for me to be escorted by a member of the Socialist Republic of Vietnam to show me the many sites and museums dedicated to the wars of the Vietnamese with the French and Americans. The tour would be that afternoon. They then briefed me on what they knew of Hanoi, and I could tell it was not the first time they had been asked to do so.

Hanoi, the capital of Vietnam and the country's second largest city, is over 1,000 years old. Lying on the banks of the Red River, Hanoi has many scenic lakes and it is sometimes referred to as the "city of lakes." Its population is about ten million for the metropolitan and rural areas. From 1954 to 1976, Hanoi was the capital of North Vietnam, and it became the capital of a reunified Vietnam in 1976. Since then, it has gradually opened its country, and now tourism from the West was an important resource. As I looked around at the many Brits, Aussies, Germans, and the few Americans in the restaurant, it was obvious that Hanoi now viewed America and other democracies with a different point of view.

The sergeants then told me I was in for a treat, as my tour would include the infamous Hanoi Hilton, "B-52 in the Lake," Ho Chi Minh's crypt and parade grounds, and the statue that depicts John McCain's crash and capture in West Lake in downtown Hanoi. I told them I was looking forward to it.

After a very good lunch of good ol' American steak and fries with beer chasers, we walked back to the compound. I was to be picked up at 1330 hours for my guided tour. After lunch, Sgt. Pope suggested I should visit Lenin Square and the Military History Museum, which was around the corner from Det. 2.

After returning to Det. 2, I walked over to Lenin Square to discover that it was just that, a big square block-long park with a statue of Lenin in the middle. I thought it was a great monument to absolute failure, but what did I know? I don't think the Vietnamese felt any different; it was an object from their past as well. Directly across the street behind yellow concrete walls was the military museum.

The Vietnam Military History Museum was established 17 July 1956, but to tour the grounds it is evident that it is largely devoted to the "American War." Virtually every type of U.S. military hardware was on display, including helicopters, tanks, armored personnel carriers, howitzers, and fighter aircraft. Each display had a brass plaque that described the armament and the date of its capture; all were taken from the South Vietnamese, when the NVA invaded the South in 1975.

In the center of the grounds, encircled by the displays was a large sculpture composed of parts of American aircraft, with a B25 bomber residing in the middle, its tail jutting up and out of the sculpture. The plaque describes the display as containing debris from F4s, F111s, B25s, B52s and other fighters, all shot down in wars dating as far back to Dien Bien Phu and the French defeat of 1954. In the front of the sculpture is a framed photo of a Vietnamese woman dragging an F111 wing from a crash scene during the "American War."

As I left the museum and walked back to Det. 2, I thought the whole museum was one big propaganda sham meant to depict the defeat of America at the hands of the brave North Vietnamese Army. Not quite true. In 1995, the Vietnamese government reported their estimate of NVA and Viet Cong fighters killed during the war at 1.1 million.

When I returned to the Det. 2 compound, my Socialist Republic guide was waiting and I was soon off to see the other historical sites. Our first stop was the Hanoi Hilton.

Located next to the lavish Somerset Grand Hanoi Hotel in downtown Hanoi is Hoa Lo Prison. The name Hoa Lo is commonly translated as "fiery furnace," or even "Hell's hole." In 1886, the prison was constructed by the French to hold Vietnamese prisoners, particularly political prisoners. A 1913 renovation expanded its capacity from 460 inmates to 600, a figure that would rise to 895 in 1922 and 1,430 in 1933. Until 1954, the French held more than 2,000 people in subhuman conditions at the prison.

Beginning in early 1967, a new area of the prison was opened for incoming American POWs, and it quickly became known as the Hanoi Hilton. The "Hilton" was used extensively during the war to house, torture, and interrogate captured servicemen, mostly American pilots shot down during bombing raids.

Today, the prison is a museum dedicated to the suffering and bravery of the Vietnamese people at the hands of the French and Americans. In the portion of the prison dedicated to the French, life sized statuary depicts Vietnamese, mainly women, starving and chained to their beds in a tortured state. In other small, dark cells, prisoners lay on concrete floors chained to their beds, displayed in brutal solitary confinement.

A smaller portion of the prison is dedicated to the "American War" and is for the exhibition of photos of U.S.

airmen who "bombed the innocent people of Vietnam," and then were captured after being shot down. The photos are painful to look at because of the obvious duress the pilots were under. In large, glass cases, POW prison garb, and the few toiletries they were allowed to possess are also displayed. Another case shows the flight suit, helmet, maps and personal effects from Senator John McCain, whose capture and imprisonment were highlighted in photos. In still another glass display there were newspaper articles and photos glorifying Jane Fonda and other American anti-war protestors.

I left the prison quickly with a bad taste in my mouth, knowing that this now popular tourist attraction was truthfully nothing more than an ugly tribute to torture. It was as if the torture of Vietnamese by the French was a justification for the Vietnamese to do it to Americans. Hoa Lo Prison is a horrible little monument with a terrible history. I think the best thing that could have been done with the place was a total demolishment.

My next stop was Ho Chi Minh Parade Square and Mausoleum.

The Ho Chi Minh Mausoleum is a large memorial located in the center of Ba Dinh Square. It is where Vietminh leader, Ho Chi Minh, read the Declaration of Independence on 2 September 1945, establishing the Democratic Republic of Vietnam.

The embalmed body of Ho Chi Minh is preserved in the cooled, central hall of the mausoleum, which is protected by a military honor guard. The body lies in a glass case with dim lights. The mausoleum is closed occasionally while work is done to restore and preserve the body, but it is normally open to the public from 0900 to 1200 hours daily. I didn't go in and I felt that I missed nothing. "Uncle Ho" was not my uncle.

"B52 in the Lake" was next on the list, a site my guide told me was not to be missed. During the 1972 Christmas air raids known as Operation Linebacker II, Vietnamese soldiers in Hanoi shot down two B-52 bombers. One of these planes crashed in Hun Tiep Lake, right in the middle of a downtown neighborhood where it has remained ever since. About the size of an Olympic-sized swimming pool, Hun Tiep is not much of a lake. Surrounded by a short concrete fence, the wreckage of the B52 is clearly visible in the murky green water.

My first and final reaction to "B52 in the Lake" was to think of the Americans that were killed on the plane and of their sacrifice. As we drove off, I found the monument deeply disturbing and callous. I continued to wonder about the fate of the aircraft crew.

UNACCOUNTED

My final stop was to see where U.S. Navy aviator John McCain crashed in West Lake on October 26, 1967. McCain was shot down by an anti-aircraft missile and parachuted wounded into Trúc Bạch Lake (West Lake) nearly drowning. He was dragged out of the water and beaten by city residents angry at having seen the area laid to waste by previous U.S. attacks. He was later taken away and held at Ho Loa Prison. A small monument celebrating the downing of "Tchn Sney Ma Can" was erected at the western shore on Thanh Niên Road on the edge of the lake. Another sad "tribute" to our war effort.

It was my last stop. My "tour" of Hanoi had come to an end. I was more than relieved when it was over, as my views of the war were certainly different than theirs. It was very apparent that both countries and people carried deep scars from that period and each had their own perspective of how the war was fought.

Chapter 41

EDGE OF THE QUE SON

Narrative: *M. McDonald-Low*

7–8 March 2012

The next afternoon I flew to Danang, and as promised, "Huey" had a sign with my name on it and was waiting for me with one of the red-star-flagged Mitsubishis. I settled in for the drive, and before I knew it, we were leaving Danang and the sprawl of the city behind us, traveling south into the farmlands and countryside along Highway One.

Vietnam began to resemble the land I remembered.

Women with black pajamas wearing coolie hats worked the rice paddies that stretched out from both sides of the two-lane highway. A boy with a stick was herding a water buffalo and her calf into a small wooden corral that sat next to a ramshackle house made of boards nailed haphazardly together. As we slowed for the many scooters and bicycles, I noticed the house had a corrugated tin roof with a small smokestack. There were two old women squatted out front talking, their coolie hats tilted back. I'm sure they were chewing betel nut as their lips were stained red.

Along the way, every two or three miles we would pass billboards erected near the highway. They usually showed a smiling child, a woman farmer, a man in a hardhat, and a soldier all set against a red background. The scene was to depict the harmony and effort of all the people working together for a better Vietnam. It was a harsh reminder to me that I was truly in a socialist country. I wondered if all of the people felt as happy and united as they were shown on the billboards.

One hour later, I arrived at Tam Ky, population 59,000 and the capital of Quang Nam Province. It was not like Danang. Tam Ky was not experiencing a growth of new buildings, and it looked run down with many older buildings still showing battle damage from the war. As we continued down the dirt road to our hotel, I looked east and saw the peaks of the lush, green mountains of the Que Son Valley. I was finally back in my AO and very close to 1165.

When I arrived at the hotel, the team was busy unpacking their gear that had finally arrived. A big truck had delivered fourteen large sealed containers of equipment from the C-17 Globemaster, and for the teams it was time for them to get organized for their eighteen missions ahead.

Jessica had told me before that while we were at the hotel we were always on our own, as the major and his Mitsubishis only showed up when there was a dinner, a place to travel to, or a mission to conduct. While the team was busy, I went looking for a café and food.

I found what I was looking for right down the street when I spotted a sign pointing down a small alley. The sign was simple and universal; it said Café. Twenty steps later I came to a small courtyard that had about a dozen picnic style tables with benches on one side and a small bar opposite them across the court. There were large, potted plants positioned throughout the courtyard along with hanging plants in the dining area. The only people in the café were three young Vietnamese women sitting together at one of the tables. I sat down and waited. The women at the table were chatting in that singsong Vietnamese that I remembered. They were also laughing and giggling the way only Asian women can. I felt I was the object of their amusement as they were stealing glances at me as they talked. Then one of the women stood up, went to the bar, grabbed a menu and brought it to me. Across her white t-shirt was a large Tiger Beer emblem, and she had a metal button pinned on the t-shirt that had her picture with the words "Tiger Girl" above it. She looked to me to be about in her early twenties. She had long black hair, a pretty face, and bright smile.

The menu she handed to me had pictures of fish, shrimp, octopus, and other sea creatures I could not identify. I had absolutely no idea what any of the words meant. When I tried to converse she had no ability to understand me. We tried pointing and trying to make words we both could understand, but it just didn't work. I couldn't speak Vietnamese, and when she had grown up she had never seen Americans or learned English. All she could do was politely giggle and smile.

I was reluctant to point at something on the menu and hope for the best so I ordered a Tiger beer, which she understood immediately. She brought me my beer and gestured to the menu, which I responded to with a shake of my head and a smile. When she presented me with my bill I paid her with a five-dollar bill and she looked delighted.

I finished my beer and left the café knowing I had no real way of communicating with the young "new" people of Vietnam, and they were equally hard pressed to understand me. The evening passed slowly after returning to my room at the hotel. I spent most of my time reviewing my maps and thinking of what was to come. I didn't have any idea how much the terrain had changed in forty-four years, but I was confident I knew where the ambush site near the "Y" was located.

The next morning, 8 March, was the day before my mission, and it was also my 65th birthday. It was the second birthday I would have in Vietnam; the first was when I had turned twenty-one. The thought crossed my mind that perhaps destiny was at play, because I knew another dinner hosted by the major at a local restaurant was scheduled for that evening.

I spent the morning reading, and then in the afternoon visiting with Hoss as he described some of the other missions he had been on. Each mission that he recanted was always prefaced by the specific circumstances in how that particular soldier, marine or airmen had become lost. I was amazed at his ability to recall not only the battles, but also the units on both sides that were engaged. Of course, his use of "Charley" as a descriptor for every North Vietnamese unit added personality and a face to the enemy, while his favorite euphemism for American troops was "you boys."

"Charley's 2nd NVA's 3rd Regiment was thick on the hillsides of Nui Hoac Ridge. You boys faced Charley's most hardened elements and he was determined not to fail. After-Action Reports clearly document his strength and strongholds and you were outnumbered twenty to one."

It was like listening to a really good book being read to you, loudly. Before long Jess, Kerry, and Wes joined us in the lobby. They had heard Hoss's booming voice telling me his tales, and it had drawn them down from their rooms to listen. Two hours later it was time for us to head to the restaurant, which was located about one-quarter mile away in a small hotel. We walked. The evening was warm and pleasant.

When we arrived at the hotel and entered the dining room on the second floor, I was surprised to find that the major was again introducing me to another former NVA officer.

Nguyen Van Qui was wrinkled and willowy, sharp-featured, 5'3" tall, with short dark brown hair. He was wearing a khaki shirt, black pants, and black leather shoes. He had a green army soft cap on his head. His teeth were crooked and yellowed, but his eyes were bright and alert. He shook my hand, pumping it up and down as he smiled broadly at me.

Qui spoke rapidly in Vietnamese. Phong listened and then told me, "Mr. Qui is from Hanoi. He is very pleased to meet a former infantry officer, like him. He has served with the 2nd NVA Division."

I had a secret thought then cross my mind. I wondered how many of them they had tucked away for my visit?

"Phong, please tell Mr. Qui that it is an honor for me to meet him as well," I said patting the small man on his shoulder. I was getting more comfortable with this, especially after my previous encounter with Ling Pho.

Qui smiled and gestured for me to join him at the table for dinner. Qui sat beside me at dinner and we spent the next few hours talking about our families and lives. We did not talk about the war, though at one point I did ask him, "Please tell me how long you fought in the South."

Qui paused and a look of concern came over his wrinkled face. I could tell he was reminiscing about something, perhaps unpleasant.

With Phong translating every few sentences, he told me his story.

"I served seven years in the South. I came down the Ho Chi Minh Trail from my home in Hanoi. I was sixteen. It took us many weeks. On my trip down the Trail, we were bombed by a B-52 one night. Shrapnel and the concussion from the huge bombs knocked me unconscious for many minutes. When I woke, I was bleeding from my ears and nose, I had shrapnel wounds to my head, and my right arm was broken. I was also deaf. It was a most a terrifying experience. Over fifty of my comrades died that night. I couldn't hear for weeks, and I spent the next three months in a make shift field hospital along the Trail recovering. Everyone who walked the Trail was afraid of the big bombers. Of course, many years later, many of us who survived the bombings now suffer from the poison of Agent Orange."

I nodded with an understanding. I had been near those types of bombs before and I could only imagine being the target of one. Agent Orange was something I was also personally exposed to and, over the years, I had consequently suffered from that experience.

During the next hour we compared our memories about certain locations and events. It was mesmerizing to listen to him describe the many areas he had fought in, particularly locations I knew first-hand.

After listening to him describe a hill and battle that sounded very similar to my time on 922, I looked at the small man, leaned in next to him and said, "We have much in common, but to be honest, over the years it never crossed my mind how much."

Phong, after translating to Qui, listened carefully to his response and then said, "He says this meeting with you has made him think on a grander scale about the similarities of your time together at war." Phong paused as Qui spoke to him rapid fire again. "Mr. Qui says it is good to have met you and to put a real face to an American soldier."

When Phong finished speaking, Qui gave me a curt bow and then warmly shook my hand, smiling and nodding as he did.

I felt a common bond with this man. He too had become a real person to me, and not just some faceless enemy from my past.

Qui and I shared Cuoc Loi toasts with each other several times that night celebrating our being alive. As the evening drew to a close, the major surprised me when he presented me with a birthday cake for my 65th birthday. As I blew out the candles, I thought of what an interesting night it had been. I believed it was a good omen for the next day and my search for 1165.

Chapter 42

MISSION 12-2VM

Narrative: *M. McDonald-Low*

9 March 2012

9 March 2012 dawned clear and crisp. It was 0530 hours, and I was up and headed for coffee and breakfast in the lobby. I had dressed in dark green, lightweight jungle wear, and I had my Oakley jungle boots on and my 12-2VM black mission hat. My backpack had my maps and a few plastic bottles of water. I had a six-inch combat knife strapped to my side. I was ready.

My team joined me one by one for breakfast and once everyone had finished with their final cups of coffee, Favian McLaren formally briefed us all on the 1165 mission we would be conducting that day. "We will travel with the major and his team, transporting by truck approximately 30 kilometers to the hamlet of Phu Lam 2, which is in the Que Son Valley, near what was formerly LZ Center. Mr. McDonald-Low will lead our team from there selecting the route of travel from our mission starting point. I want to remind everyone that it is going to be warm out there, so bring plenty of water. Dave, you've got the heaviest load, so I want you to be particularly aware of your hydration. Kerry, you'll walk with Mr. McDonald-Low and ensure the same."

"Once we arrive on site we will be having two local Vietnamese join us who may have information on this case. When a canvas of the area was done in preparation for this mission, our Vietnamese counterparts turned up these two potential witnesses. Wes, you, Phong, and Hieu will handle the questioning. Please remember these are paid contributors and that we're looking for quality, specific info."

Favian paused and then looked at me, "Was there anything you wanted to say, Mr. McDonald-Low?"

I stood up and looked around the room at each team member and lastly at Favian, "Thank you, Favian. I want to thank everyone for joining me today. My one thought is that 1165 didn't sign up to fight in Vietnam to be left behind. Nobody did. I look forward to identifying his correct loss location."

I sounded confident, but I had butterflies in my stomach. The time had finally come for me to see if my years of dreams, recollections, research, and map coordinates would finally yield 1165's location. I wondered how much of that remote valley, hillside and trail would be the same? Looking at a map is one thing, being on the actual terrain would be a whole different beast.

The major and his team arrived with the trucks at 0900 hours. We began our journey, driving west and then north on a small dirt road that would take us to Phu Lam 2 in the valley, near what was LZ Center. When we turned west I could see the mountains of the Que Son about ten kilometers distant. The road meandered through the flat countryside where poor, small hamlets dotted the sides of the road. The people stared at our four vehicles with the many Americans inside. I am sure it was the presence of the red military flags with their yellow star insignia's that had them staring as well. They seemed both curious and cautious as they watched us pass. The infrequent scooter or water buffalo drawn cart we encountered would receive a blast of our horns if they were too slow to move out of the way. The major kept it moving until we reached the mountains where our road became smaller and more winding as it made its way towards the heart of the Que Son Valley.

The small, one lane road initially followed a stream, and the growth of vines, plants and trees became more and more lush the further we traveled. It was green and humid. It smelled as I remembered. It was the earthy, wet, chlorophyll laden, close, decaying musk of the jungle. As I looked out the window, I thought of how we used to claw our way through these areas sweating under our loads, as we moved ever so slowly and watchful. I was already thinking of the streambed along the trail, the "Y," and the scenes yet to unfold.

After a bumpy, narrow, twisting ride, we arrived at Phu Lam 2 at about 1030 hours. The first thing I did as I jumped out of the truck was to look south at Nui Hoac Ridge and Hill 352. I was standing near a spot where we had spent several night defensive positions in early May 1968. Nui Hoac towered above us, dark green and still ominous. It was larger than I remembered, as I thought of my days spent there and their cost.

I turned slowly around and surveyed the small valley and surrounding hills. It was easy to pick out where LZ Center had been located, and I could clearly see the "saddle" that dipped between it and the nearby hills. It was there that I was going. Other than a small power line I saw that followed the small dirt road through the valley, it all looked the same as it did in 1968.

I walked from the cars after grabbing my backpack, left the road, and followed a small path beside the rice paddy. It was the rice paddy that we had crossed so many times before to get to Phu Lam 2 and begin our climb up Hill 352. Dust Off had landed on the far side of the paddy to pick up our casualties. A little farther down the path, small dikes and walls led to an adjoining paddy where my platoon and company had landed on our combat air assault of 5 May. I looked at the map I was carrying and there was no doubt about it, everything had begun here. I looked across the paddy and saw that we could follow an adjoining path headed towards the base of Hill 348, LZ Center and the "saddle" next to it.

As I stood there looking at my map and glancing at the terrain, Kerry, Favian, and Hoss joined me. The rest of the team and the major and his assistants were still spread out back to the trucks slowly coming my way.

"You know where you're at, Mike?" Hoss asked as he took his hat off and wiped his brow with his handkerchief.

"Not a problem, Hoss. I know right where I am. We're headed to the right of that saddle up there," I said pointing towards the right of Hill 348.

Kerry then passed me a metal walking stick that he had just telescoped it out to its full length. "This will help on the trail ahead, Mike. Everyone has one and I thought you should, too."

"Thanks, Kerry. I'll use it," I said to him as I smiled and headed for the narrow path that would take me around the paddy to the other side.

When I reached the base of the hill after crossing around the paddy, I saw the path as it reached back into brush and jungle and started up the hill. It wasn't the trail we had followed so many years ago, but I knew it would lead to the same spot. I would just work backwards from there.

The vegetation was lush with green, broad-leafed plants, vines, small trees, bamboo and grasses. The trail was narrow and rocky at times, as it gradually climbed upwards and wove in and out of jungle growth. I paused after fifteen minutes. I was already drenched in sweat, my forehead dripping under my black hat. My lightweight nylon shirt was soaked. I could see everyone behind me still spread out on the trail, approaching my position. I had stopped in a small clearing that offered some shade and I drank some water.

Soon, everyone arrived at the clearing and also began to drink. Hoss, to my surprise still looked fresh and seemed to be hardly sweating. Jessica seemed equally ambivalent to the temperature and humidity. She had borrowed a pointed coolie hat from one of the major's men, Huey I think, and looked very comfortable, almost "dink-like" I thought. Her black under blouse, blue top shirt, and black pants looked dry and unstained from sweat as she casually sat on a rock and chatted with Wes Hanson.

After a few minutes, my body started to cool down and I headed back up the trail, my teammates following. We hiked thru thick foliage for another ten minutes when the trail widened and I could see that a tractor had plowed a small, rough road down from the top near the "saddle." I stopped. I wasn't expecting to see a road and it certainly wasn't on my maps. I continued on as the road rose up the hillside. Another 200 meters later we reached the "saddle." To the east and directly above us was the slope leading up to Hill 348 and what was LZ Center. A rocky finger came down from the hill and separated into two distinct, separate hills. The ravine between the two spread out where there was a small grassy clearing and a trail that led from it on the opposite side.

The edge of the clearing had a primitive wire gate slung across it and two beige colored cows with large horns were grazing on the grass. I wanted access to the trail I had seen, and decided after concurring with Favian that we should bypass the clearing and cows, cut our way across the hill and come up the trail that led to the clearing from the other side. I was pretty sure that would be the trail that led to the "Y."

The major, after conferring with Wes, directed two men he had brought from Phu Lam 2 to aid us and cut a trail across the hill following my directions. Twenty meters into the brush we encountered leeches. David Clark was first to notice as he had a fifty-cent sized bloodstain on his shirt. Soon others were recognizing that they too had leeches attached to their boots and clothing. I didn't have mosquito repellant and no one was a smoker, but the "Off" worked great. Just a quick spray and the leeches dropped. We all then sprayed our boots and trousers to avoid any further attacks.

The "wait-a-minute" vines were another story. I had forgotten how awful they were as they tugged and snagged at our clothing, bootlaces, and sleeves. The "wait-a-minute" vines also made us bleed from their small, sharp thorns. "Some things never change," I thought.

It took us over thirty minutes of cutting to go another fifty meters. The heat was intense and I was in a dead sweat, my body slick with perspiration. I called another halt and turned to Favian. "I've got a better idea. Let's back track to the road and go through the fence and across that clearing. We'll be here all day at this rate, and I'm pretty sure the "Y" is on the other side of that clearing down trail about seventy-five meters."

"I couldn't agree with you more, Mike. This is terrible. I'll get everyone turned around."

We arrived back at the edge of the grassy clearing fifteen minutes later and I climbed through the fence. The cows skittered away and I walked down the trail that bordered the clearing. In the middle I stopped and told Favian, "I need some time here. I want to check my maps and walk down this trail. Have everyone wait here, please."

Favian turned to the team and told everyone to take "10." My team members dropped their packs and gear, as did the major and his men. I took off my pack, grabbed my map and walking stick and headed out of the clearing down the small, rocky trail. It curved to the right as the bush closed in on either side. Fifteen meters further down the trail it turned gradually to the right at a flat, rocky spot, and then headed steeply down towards the valley. At the juncture where it turned, I stopped and turned around. Directly ahead of me I could see a small, partially hidden entrance that concealed an old trail. I walked over closer and pushed some of leaves and plants aside. The trail led straight over and down to the valley on the far side. I had reached the "Y."

I stood there and looked again at my map, but I knew exactly where I was, and where I had stood forty-four years earlier. The trail leading back up to the clearing was the one I had sent 1165 up that morning in May. For me, it was as sharp and clear as if it had happened yesterday.

Chapter 43

"X" MARKS THE SPOT

Narrative: *M. McDonald-Low*

9 March 2012

I walked back up to where I had last remembered seeing 1165. It was just past the bend in the trail where I had lost sight of him. From there I walked slowly towards the grassy clearing on the trail as I counted to fifteen. By the time I reached fifteen, I was ten meters into the grassy clearing, in the middle of where my teammates were waiting for my return. I then walked back to the "Y" and did it again. As I reached my count of fifteen again, I called over to Favian and asked him to confirm my coordinates of BT067254 with his GPS device. Twenty seconds later he confirmed that I was on the exact spot. As soon as Favian confirmed my location, he called everyone over.

"We have confirmation of the location from Mr. McDonald-Low, and it has been verified on my GPS. Dave, go ahead and prepare your gear and let's conduct a thorough search of this immediate vicinity."

Dave Clark, our EOD expert, already had his metal detector out and was starting its calibration. As he finished, he unpacked his backpack and pulled out dozens of small red flags mounted on stiff wire. Each was about twelve inches long. He put them into a pouch and slung it over his neck and right arm.

Dave started his sweep on the trail at the bend and expanded it methodically as he reached the grassy area beside the trail. He had his headphones on and was listening for hits. As he started sweeping back and forth I saw him stop almost immediately and mark a location with a red flag. He continued on and before long there were a number of flags dotting the grassy area as it fell off towards a small, heavily-brushed ravine.

As Dave was sweeping with his metal detector, Wes Hanson called me over to where he stood. I listened as he questioned the two older Vietnamese men who supposedly had information about 1165. Phong and Hieu translated. After about five minutes of back and forth conversation Phong told us, "These two men remember an American soldier being left behind in this area. They are not sure where exactly, nor do they have a year. One is from the village of Phu Lam and the other is from a small village on the other side of this hill. I do not think they can help us."

The two Vietnamese continued talking with Wes and Phong, who were now asking pointed questions about year and specific locations. Neither of the Vietnamese could agree on a year or any detail that could aid us. Wes told me that this was the case many times with Vietnamese witnesses. It was just too long ago and they had witnessed too many incidents in this area.

I turned away and watched Dave as he continued to plant his flags. I then walked over to where Hoss stood next to the gate where we had entered the clearing. He was looking back towards Dave and down on the small grassy field. When I reached him he said, "Mike, this is a beautiful area for an ambush. Look at the fields of fire Charley had as those boys of yours came around that bend."

Hoss then pointed to the elevated finger on our left, which extended down from LZ Center. A small ravine separated it from the grassy area and another hill with dense brush, which ran up to the right. "If 1165 was killed where you say, it was easy to see how they weren't able to retrieve him when those boys from 1-6 Infantry came down. They got the other two because they were closer and ahead of 1165. He was just too far down the clearing for them to get to. I would also say that when Charley buried him it was probably close to or in that ravine. The hills to the right and to the left are inconvenient, and they would be right in the way of where they were operating. They wanted him out of the way. Given the natural slope here to the ravine, his remains will have washed and worked their way downhill over the years."

Hoss continued as he walked back towards the clearing, "The NVA were thick in here, Mike. They were operating here all of the time, and they would have never left a body exposed. There's too great a chance for disease, and Charley always buried the dead, usually in a shallow, surface grave. They just didn't leave bodies lying around on their turf. Of course, they would have stripped the body of any useful gear or clothing before burying him."

As Hoss and I reached the clearing, I watched Favian, Jessica, and Kerry probing the areas where the red flags were located. Each used a bayonet and gently probed all around each flag. To my delight, the flag closest to my coordinates yielded an M79 grenade shell and a large piece of shrapnel. Rusty and caked with red clay from over forty years of burial, the shell casing was as good as a diamond to me. 1165 had been an M79 grenadier, and I was hopeful the casing was his. Paul, our team photographer, took pictures documenting the location of the find, and afterwards Favian presented the shell casing and shrapnel to me. I put them in my pack along with some dirt from where they had been buried. I believed that I finally had a piece of concrete evidence from his location.

No other items of interest were discovered next to any of the other flags. The team started to pack up as Hoss finished his survey and notes. Dave had pulled all of his flags except the one from the location of the shell casing. I asked Favian to join me as I held a POW/MIA flag that I had brought with me from Ray's office. Favian and I held it over the small red flag as Paul took our picture. I then pulled the red flag and invited my entire JPAC team and the major and his assistants, to join us for one last photo.

My investigative mission to find and pinpoint 1165's real location was over. My job was done. It would now be up to JPAC to examine all of the information our IT-1 would provide.

As I walked out of the grassy clearing, I stopped and looked across at Nui Hoac Ridge and Hill 352. I thought of all the men on both sides who had fought and died there and how our struggles during those six days I would forever carry with me. I then thought again of 1165 as I patted the grenade shell casing in my backpack.

I looked back one last time at the grassy clearing and thought of how close I was to 1165 this day. I then crossed through the fence and started down the rough road to begin the trek back to our vehicles. After forty-four years, I knew the mystery of 11 May 1968, had come to an end for me. I was also transformed from the experience, and I felt the weight of Vietnam begin to lighten on my shoulders.

Chapter 44

RESURRECTIONS' END

Narrative: *Clifford Van Artsdalen - MIA 1165*
9 March 2012

As the fog and mist of the Que Son evaporated in the morning heat, I vividly recalled how it all ended that morning in May. And since that moment, nothing. Nothing until this morning when I had remembered it all. Every detail.

How could I forget "Pennsylfuckingvania" and talking with my high school friends about "killin' slopes in the Nam"? Then my rush through basic and advanced infantry training at Ft. Benning, and meeting Roosevelt Clay. If that wasn't enough, we ended up shipping off to the same unit, the 11th Brigade, in of all places, Hawaii.

Hawaii. I had spent more time training in Hawaii than I did fighting in Vietnam. Sgt. Hodges, the LT, Big Todd Lockhart, Gates, Zapata, they didn't realize how good it had been to be in the Kahuka's "playing" war. Nobody dies when you "play" war. No one gets head shot, no one has their guts blown out by a grenade, and no one dies in an ambush.

UNACCOUNTED

Real war is waiting to die. In Delta Company, we were all just waiting to be placed in a position where the odds sooner or later would dictate that we would die or come damn close to it. LZ Leslie, LZ Center, Hill 922, LZ Ross, LZ Baldy, Hill 352, the Que Son, Nui Hoac Ridge; they were all just dead zones waiting to consume both sides. Each place took its toll, as it erased my friends and their replacements one by one.

I thought of the many men of Delta and the way that they had departed; some simply dead and gone, others agonizing from their wounds and taking a Dust Off "back to the world." Cpt. Marks had been on his way "back to world" and had never made it. It hadn't been a great way for the company to start, and it certainly was a sign of bad things to come.

I remembered how easy it had been to shrug-off the loss of friends, but not really. I had said, "Ain't no big thang" so many times I actually started to believe it. I believed it right up to the moment Roosevelt died. Roosevelt: the memory of my best friend made me happy, and then it saddened me. Not that he was the first or last of my friends from Hawaii to die, Roosevelt was simply one of the best of them, and my endearing "brother."

Lockhart and Zapata were the last of my friends to die. I wondered how many others had survived? This thought strengthened in me when I had begun to distinguish a new, yet familiar presence when the men arrived today. This too was a part of me. A fragment. I didn't know why, but it somehow felt right to have them here. There was also a familiarity to one of them that comforted me, and I lingered on the sensation when the man walked, stopped, and then headed down the trail we both knew. It was the trail that led to the "Y" and the terrible things that happened there.

The man paused and stood there.

I could also feel the others who were waiting on the man. Suddenly, a question flooded my thoughts, "Why? Why was I still here?" The thought was new and haunting. It was also confusing to me.

For the very, very long time that I had been here, nothing. And now this. I felt a wave of uncertainty and apprehension begin to seize and then strangle me. The enormity of the "why" consumed me as I now sensed a new excitement in the men. Something had happened.

Then there was a quiet.

I dwelled on these thoughts until I detected the men beginning to leave. The familiarity and comfort of their presence had seemed fleeting to me. As the last of the men departed, the one man stopped and paused for a moment. It was during that instant a deep emptiness washed over me and then ever so briefly, a sense of hope ran through me.

UNACCOUNTED

As the man left, I could feel my thoughts and memories begin to dwindle and fade. I attempted to grasp them, but they slowly slid away from me. I sensed the shadows drawing longer and the day began to quietly wither away.

As the darkness crept over me, my thoughts stilled, and then I finally rested.

Chapter 45

HOMEWARD

Narrative: *M. McDonald-Low*

9-13 March 2012

I walked slowly off the hill and looked back at LZ Center. It was as it always was to me, a place I had never been; as the saying goes "so close, yet so far away." I then turned my attention back across the valley to Nui Hoac Ridge and Hill 352. I knew this would be the last time I would look at that infamous terrain.

The ride back to Tam Ky was quiet, each of us filled with our own thoughts of the day. When we returned to the hotel I felt exuberant and exhausted.

Jessica must have noticed something in my expression when we were walking in because she tapped me on the shoulder and said, "You okay? You seem lost in thought."

"No, I'm good. It was a long day. I'm surprised by how little everything had changed in forty plus years. Even the leeches were still there. It was strange for me to be back on that trail, especially at the "Y." I am still coming to grips with that."

"I understand, totally. Each of us can relate. We put so much research and work into these cases it becomes personal. When we have an American witness like you with us, it becomes even more so. All of us admire your service in Vietnam and when we come here, I am always in awe of how you were able to even operate in the jungle. I can't imagine."

"Thanks, Jess. It crossed my mind today as well. It reminded me of how young we were, and how much older I am now."

"Not too old to still hump." It was Kerry offering a bit of infantry humor to the moment as he walked up and stood next to Jess and me.

"Thanks, Kerry. It takes one to know one," I said with a smile.

"Yes, it does."

Over the next fifteen minutes each of my teammates thanked me for my participation in the search and we began our goodbyes. I would be leaving the next morning for my flights to Hawaii and home, and they would be off on their next mission. I had grown fond of these wonderful people and their dedication and professionalism to their mission of "Until they are Home." I could not have had a more supportive group with me on my quest.

The next morning the major drove me to the Danang airport for the first leg of my journey home, Bangkok, Thailand. After he dropped me off and we said our brief, polite goodbyes, I reflected that for someone I had just spent five days with, I knew little about him. He was an enigma.

12 and 13 March I traveled from Bangkok to Narita, Japan, where I caught my flight to Hawaii. On that last, long leg of my journey, I revisited my tour in Vietnam, beginning with Hanoi. Hanoi was stuck in my mind. It was certainly the most disappointing portion of my trip. I couldn't wrap my head around their monuments to torture, inhumanity and dishonesty. It was government propaganda and deceit at its worst. Conversely, it was the Vietnamese people who provided me with some of the most positive experiences of my journey. I also sensed that for the first time in a long while, I felt more complete. My memories of Vietnam were now no longer singularly wrapped in the brutal packaging of war. I felt satisfied about my contributions to the mission and more importantly, for fulfilling my duty to find 1165 - Clifford Van Artsdalen.

When the plane made its descent into Honolulu, I mused that this time on my return from Vietnam, there were no demons inside my head traveling with me. I also knew that there would be no angry demonstrators calling me a murderer at the airport. Good stuff.

UNACCOUNTED

I arrived in Hawaii at 0723 hours. It felt great to be back in America, especially a friendly one. I spent two more days in Hawaii going through my mission debrief at JPAC with Ray, and catching up on the time zone changes before returning home to my family in Petaluma, California.

My mission to investigate and find the location of 1165 was just about over. I wanted to check all of my research one more time.

Chapter 46

CONFIRMATION
M. McDonald-Low
March – June 2012

EMAIL

Favian McLaren JPAC, to Michael McDonald-Low

13 Mar 2012

Michael,

I trust your return to Hawaii went well. I just want to sincerely thank you for helping us set the record straight and helping us to correctly locate 1165.

Stay in touch and I'll look you up when I visit California again!

r/s,

Favian

———

EMAIL

Michael McDonald-Low to Favian McLaren, JPAC

16 Mar 2012

Favian,

It was a pleasure meeting you and working with your terrific team. I enjoyed everyone's professionalism and care. It was a great honor for me to be involved.

FYI: Thought you would want to know that when I returned to Hawaii I made a mental note to remind you that 1165 was a grenadier – he carried a 40mm grenade launcher on the day of the incident. The 40mm casing we found may be relevant to him. I relayed this info to Ray Carne when I saw him. We shall see.

Thanks again, Chief. I will never forget my time there with you, Jess, Hoss, Dave, Paul, Wes, Kerry, Howard, Mr. Button and our two wonderful interpreters, especially Phong.

Sincerely,

Michael McDonald-Low

————

EMAIL

Michael McDonald-Low to Ray Carne JPAC J2

4 June 2012

Ray,

Please refer to my email of 28 Sept 2010, where it references the 1/6 Infantry AAR...."Late in the morning of May 11, 1968, a valiant effort of A/1-6, 198th Infantry would recover two of the three soldiers of D/1-20 killed vicinity BT067253. Heavy enemy resistance made it impossible for them to retrieve one soldier."

Here's also what was in their After-Action Report concerning another casualty at that location… I just discovered this … "Mid-morning on 11 May 1968, elements of A/1-6 moved eastward from LZ Center toward the area where soldiers from D/1-20 had been cut off. At 1111 hours, 11 May 1968, A/1-6 made contact with the enemy at BT065254. They had just entered a draw and spotted D/1-20 (corrected) soldiers killed in an ambush previously, when the enemy opened up on them. They had 2 WHA at BT067253 from automatic weapons' fire and small arms' fire. By 1227 hours, one of the wounded men died (2LT Lee Marconi), and one NVA had been killed and an AK-47 captured."

Note the coordinates of Marconi's death. It is same ambush location as 1165. This is solid documentation and further supports my loss site location.

Michael

––––––

EMAIL
Ray Carne JPAC, to Michael McDonald-Low
13 June 2012

Michael,

I have re-verified the information that you have sent me, and this new info further confirms your location for 1165. We have all we need to move forward. I will keep you updated on progress in the future.

Thanks again for your service and commitment!

Ray

EPILOGUE

Though I frequently think of Clifford Van Artsdalen and the events that occurred during that period in 1968, I now rarely dream of Vietnam, being in combat, or the morning of 11 May.

My mission to Vietnam changed me; it gave a face and a soul to my former enemy and stripped me of some of the anger I carried with me for the last forty plus years. On the other hand, it didn't leave me forgetful of my experiences or lessen my disdain for the enemies of the United States.

I had never seen Vietnam at peace or the people so confident in their day-to-day life without the violence of war looming over them. In retrospect, I do believe if they had a choice and could have changed it all, Vietnam would be free today. Nonetheless, the Vietnamese people, particularly those in what was South Vietnam seem somewhat apathetic to the weighty chains of socialistic rule, and they have thrived. Ultimately, it was capitalism that became our best weapon in Vietnam, and the transformation is just beginning to take hold.

UNACCOUNTED

I am eternally grateful to be part of the mission to find MIA 1165, and I continue to ardently work on his case to see him eventually returned home.

The mission stated by the new Defense POW/MIA Accounting Agency reads, "Provide the fullest possible accounting for our missing personnel to their families and the nation." This is easier said than done.

One of the biggest challenges facing the Defense POW/MIA Accounting Agency will be the development of an aggressive plan of action to speed-up and streamline the process between research, investigation, and excavation. There are hundreds of MIA cases that are still being researched. Those that have completed research are now pending an Investigation Decision Board to approve an on-site survey in Southeast Asia. Many other Southeast Asia MIA files have completed the investigation and survey process, but are now waiting for an Excavation Decision Board. In 2015, there were a significant number of Southeast Asia MIAs that had been approved for excavation, but the great majority of these excavations have not been scheduled due to a lack of funding and personnel. Many of these cases have been backlogged a considerable length of time.

As of November 2015, over 1,600 U.S. soldiers, Marines, and airmen are still missing in action in Vietnam, Laos, and Cambodia. The hopes for the recovery of these men diminish each day, as the corrosive soil and climate of Southeast Asia gradually degrade the last bits of evidence and remains. It is extraordinarily important that America becomes more acutely aware of our MIAs and the importance of the mission to ultimately account for them. Until then, they remain unaccounted.

END

ACKNOWLEDGEMENTS /

CREDITS

Unaccounted was not originally intended to be a book. It began as notes and emails in 2009, as I began my research into the fate of Clifford Van Artsdalen. These accumulated pieces of information evolved into a briefing I prepared for JPAC in 2012.

Almost four years later, with the help of family and many friends, *Unaccounted* became a reality. It was a terribly slow process, gut wrenching and not without pain. There were many times I had reached a point where I felt I could go no further, only to remember that I had a duty to complete it. Along the way I finished it in many different lengths and versions, only to remain ultimately dissatisfied. I apologize to my friends and sons who endured these early attempts and for their kind reviews. They ultimately helped me make it the book it is today.

In retrospect, the hardest part for me was to attempt to graphically describe and emotionally relate to the terrible injuries and circumstances of death we all experienced. I had grown so accustomed to turning a blind eye and switching myself off in Vietnam, I didn't realize that it would affect my writing the same way, forty years later. I apparently had truly embraced "Ain't no big thang" as a lifelong emotional cushion.

I sincerely hope I did a worthy job of portraying our little piece of the war and the men who served with me, particularly Clifford Van Artsdalen.

Of course, I would like to sincerely thank the people of the POW/MIA community who played such an important role in the search for 1165, and in particular: Camille, Ray, Bob, Hoss, Favian, Wes, Jessica and Kerry. Best of the best.

I also would like to personally call out the following people who provided me inspiration, encouragement and important input over the years during my struggle to write this book. I am forever grateful and couldn't have done it without each of you.

MDavid and Sheridan Low – My two sons gave me the push to keep going and to make this a personal story. They also helped me decide the very best way to present the story and were a constant source of encouragement. Sheridan was also responsible for the great cover design.

Jayne Marchesi – Editor, friend and companion, Jayne was meticulous, patient and provided me with some amazing insight; she made this book consistently better.

UNACCOUNTED

Michael Gates – Long time friend, Mike provided me with a sense of humor and no matter how big the task originally looked, he made it seem doable. For his contributions, I used his name for a great sergeant in 1st Squad.

Patrick McIntyre – Vietnam veteran and high school friend, Pat reminded me of the sacrifice and duty of the men we served with and to portray them honestly. Cocoa was his story, and out of respect, I borrowed his name for my RTO. Pat was also one of my faithful early advisors on content flow.

Brad Kotsaris – Friend and confidant, Brad always said I was on the right track even when the work was rough and unfinished. I used his name for Delta's company medic as a tribute.

Ron Corbin – Vietnam veteran, helicopter pilot, Hamburger Hill combatant, and author, Ron had the thankless job of originally proofing my story and providing me insight about presenting it properly.

Todd Lockhart – Iraq and Afghanistan combat infantry veteran, Todd provided me insight and accuracy on 11B10s and their duties, and reminded me that PTSD was not limited to Vietnam vets. Out of respect, I used his name for a key member of 1st Squad.

Mike Williams – High school friend and a former West Pointer, Mike kept me on track with the language of the 60s.

Tom Abel – Vietnam veteran and buddy from high school, Tom helped me believe what I was doing was important, and that it was necessary for people to know the story.

CREDITS

*Information on 2nd NVA Division units, officers and general information on the Que Son and Hiep Duc Valleys credit: James F. Humphries, *Through the Valley, Vietnam, 1967-1968*; published by Lynne Rienner Publishers, Boulder, CO, 1999. Used with permission of the publisher. This is a terrific blow-by-blow tale of the brave men of the 196th Light Infantry Brigade in the Hiep Duc and Que Son Valley.

All excerpts from historical After-Action Reports are credited to 1/6th Infantry, 198th LIB - www.a-1-6.org, LZ Center - www.lzcenter.com and the personnel who have superbly maintained these historical documents.

VIETNAM TERMINOLOGY

A1 Skyraider: propeller-driven fighter. The A-1 was a primary close air support aircraft for the USAF and VNAF during the Vietnam War.

AA: anti-aircraft artillery.

ARVN: soldier in the Army of the Republic of South Vietnam.

Air Cav: air cavalry, referring to helicopter-borne infantry.

AK-47: (also AK or Kalashnikov) rifle. The AK-47 was the basic infantry weapon of the North Vietnamese Army (NVA) and the Vietcong (VC). Originally manufactured by the Soviet Union, most of these assault rifles used in the war were made in the People's Republic of China, which was the major supplier of armaments to NVA and VC forces.

AO: area of operations.

Battalion: a battalion is an organizational institution in the Army and is commanded by a lieutenant colonel. An infantry battalion usually had around 900 people and an artillery battalion about 500 people. During the Vietnam War, American battalions were usually much smaller.

Birds: helicopters.

Bouncing Betty: a WWII explosive device that propels upward about four feet into the air and then detonates.

Brigade: the term "brigade" is a basic military organizational institution. During the Vietnam War, a division was organized into three brigades, with each brigade commanded by a colonel. A division consists of approximately 20,000 people. There were also separate infantry brigades functioning in the Vietnam War. The 196th, and 198th Infantry Brigades fought in the war until 1967, when they were joined by the 11th Infantry Brigade, and the three were brought together to form the Americal Division, or the 23rd Infantry.

C4: a very stable plastic explosive carried by infantry soldiers. Lightweight, stable, C4 had a potent explosive power. Malleable with a texture similar to play dough, it could be formed into a shaped charge of infinite configuration. Because it could be safely burned, C4 was popular with GIs, who would break off a small piece of it for heating water or C-rations.

CA: combat air assault - an operation in which assault forces are inserted by helicopter assets to engage and destroy enemy forces or to seize and hold key terrain.

CAL: caliber.

CBU: see cluster bombs.

UNACCOUNTED

Charles or Sir Charles: the term is inclusive of Viet Cong and North Vietnamese Army forces.

ChiCom: a term describing a weapon manufactured in China.

Chinook: the CH-47 cargo helicopter; also called "Shithook" or "Hook."

Claymore Mine: a popular, fan-shaped, antipersonnel land mine. Widely used in Vietnam, the Claymore antipersonnel mine was designed to produce a directionalized, fan-shaped pattern of fragments.

Close Air Support: air strikes against enemy targets that are close to friendly forces.

Cluster Bombs / CBU: one-pound, baseball-sized bombs were usually dropped in lots of 600 or more. The bomblets were released from a dispenser in such a way as to spread them across a wide area. The most popular was the CBU-49, a canister of time-delayed bomblets that would go off randomly over a thirty-minute period, each blasting out 250 white-hot ball bearings.

Company, Rifle Company Organization: in the 11th Light Infantry Brigade, each Rifle Company originally had three rifle platoons and a weapons platoon. (In Vietnam, the men in the weapons platoon were quickly redistributed to the rifle platoons to compensate for casualties.) The three rifle platoons were normally composed of forty to forty-two soldiers.

Contact: condition of being in contact with the enemy, exchanging fire.

Crew Chief: Huey crewmember who maintains the aircraft.

Dink: what the grunts referred to all Vietnamese as, denoting their smaller stature.

Doc: what the grunts would call medics.

Dust Off: a nickname for a medical evacuation helicopter or mission. Also, see "Medevac."

Elephant Grass: tall, sharp-edged grass found in the highlands of Vietnam.

Eleven Bravo / 11B: nickname for 11B10; MOS designation for an infantryman.

ETA: estimated time of arrival.

F4 Phantom – two seat, twin-engine fighter jet that provided close air support for infantry as well as flying interceptor and recon missions.

Fast Movers: term used to describe jets.

Fire Base: sometimes called a fire support base, temporary artillery firing position often secured by infantry.

Fighting Pit: a hasty defensive position, typically prepared for three infantrymen; a trench dug to a depth of 3-4 feet, approximately 6-8 feet in length and 2-3 feet wide.

FO: artillery forward observer.

UNACCOUNTED

Foxhole: a hasty defensive position, typically prepared for one infantryman; a hole or small trench dug to a depth of 3-4 feet.

FNG: Fucking New Guy – term used to describe soldiers newly arrived in Vietnam or those of little experience.

Green Tracers: color of the ammunition fired from enemy weapons whereby you could track/trace its path.

Grunt: a popular nickname for an infantryman in Vietnam; supposedly derived from the sound one made from lifting up his rucksack.

Gunship: an armed, offensive helicopter used for air protection of slicks or close air support for infantry.

HE: high explosive.

Hooch: a thatch hut: interior fire pit for cooking, typically one room 10' x 15', some larger with a separate, smaller room attached.

Hot: dangerous, such as a hot LZ (where aircraft are receiving enemy fire).

HQ: headquarters.

Huey: called the "Iroquois" by the United States Army, the aircraft is much better known by its nickname of "Huey," derived from its initial designation of HU-1. Three combat troops normally rode on each side of the aircraft, and through the wide open doors could exit quickly, greatly reducing the time the helicopter was on the ground.

Hump: to slog around on foot.

I Corps: northernmost military region in South Vietnam.

Incoming: receiving enemy mortar or rocket fire.

In Country: Vietnam.

Insertion: helicopter placement of combat troops in an operational area.

Jungle Canopy: thick jungle, plants growing at three levels - ground level, intermediate, and tree-top height.

KIA: Killed In Action.

KHA: Killed Hostile Action

KP: kitchen police (clean-up).

LAW: M72 Light Antitank Weapon. A shoulder-fired, 66mm rocket with a one-time, disposable fiberglass launcher.

LRP OR LRRP: (Lurp) long-range reconnaissance patrol. 4, 6, or 8 man teams.

LT: lieutenant.

LZ: landing zone.

M16: the standard American rifle used in Vietnam after 1966.

M60: American-made 7.62mm (.308 cal) machine gun.

M79: single-barreled, break-action grenade launcher, which fired 40mm projectiles, or buckshot rounds.

Mad Minute: concentrated fire of all weapons for a brief period of time.

Medevac: medical evacuation by helicopter; also called an "Evac" or "Dust Off."

MIA: Missing In Action.

MHA: Missing Hostile Action.

NVA: North Vietnamese Army, also PAVN - Peoples Army of Vietnam.

P-38: can opener for C-rations.

Point: lead soldier in a unit.

Poncho Liner: nylon insert to the military rain poncho, used as a blanket in Vietnam.

Pop Smoke: to mark a target or Landing Zone (LZ) with a smoke grenade.

PRC-25: lightweight infantry field radio, nicknamed the Prick.

Recon: reconnaissance.

RTO: radio telephone operator or radioman who carried the PRC-25.

Ruck or Rucksack: aluminum framed, nylon backpack issued to infantry in Vietnam.

Search and Destroy: offensive operations designed to find and destroy enemy forces.

Sitrep: situation report.

Six: infantry term for commanding officers; Six / Company Commander, One Six / 1st Platoon Leader, Two Six / 2nd Platoon Leader, etc.

Slick: helicopter used to lift troops or cargo - they carried only protective armament systems.

Spooky or Puff the Magic Dragon: C-47 gunship - 7.62 mini guns mounted in side windows.

Stand-Down: period of rest and refitting in which all operational activity, except for security, is stopped.

Top: slang term for Platoon Sergeant or Company First Sergeant.

VC: Viet Cong guerilla forces.

WHA: Wounded Hostile Action.

WIA: Wounded In Action.

THE AUTHOR

Michael McDonald-Low graduated from Officers Candidate School at Ft. Knox, Kentucky, in July 1966, where he was commissioned as a 2nd Lieutenant at nineteen years of age. He served in Vietnam in 1967 and 1968 as a 1st Lieutenant infantry platoon leader and later as company commander after being promoted to Captain. He has been working with the Department of Defense and their search for Clifford Van Artsdalen - MIA 1165 since 2009.

Among his military awards and decorations are the Combat Infantryman's Badge, Bronze Star with "V" Device for Heroism, Bronze Star for Meritorious Service, Purple Heart with Oak Leaf Cluster (2), Army Commendation Medal, Meritorious Service Medal (2x), National Defense Service Medal, Vietnam Presidential Unit Citation, Vietnam Gallantry Cross Unit Citation, Vietnam Civil Action Honor Medal, Southeast Asia Service Medal, Army Valorous Unit Award, Army Good Conduct Award, Republic of Vietnam Campaign Medal, and the Tet Counter-Offensive Medal.

In September 2014, McDonald-Low joined the newly reorganized Defense POW/MIA Accounting Agency (DPAA) as its first-ever Southeast Asia Veteran Liaison. As the Southeast Asia Veteran Liaison, he participates in MIA case analysis and review of existing DPAA background information and investigative reporting related to unresolved ground loss cases in Vietnam, Laos, and Cambodia.

CPSIA information can be obtained
at www.ICGtesting.com
Printed in the USA
LVOW13s1804020217
522956LV00053B/703/P